A
Short Guide
to
WRITING
ABOUT LITERATURE

A
Short Guide
to
WRITING
ABOUT LITERATURE

SYLVAN BARNET
TUFTS UNIVERSITY

LITTLE, BROWN AND COMPANY
BOSTON

FIRST PRINTING

Published simultaneously in Canada
by Little, Brown & Company (Canada) Limited

PRINTED IN THE UNITED STATES OF AMERICA

ACKNOWLEDGMENTS

The author gratefully acknowledges permission to use excerpts from works by the following authors:

Adams, Robert M. (p. 81). Reprinted from "Ibsen on the Contrary," in *Modern Drama*, edited by Anthony Caputi (New York: W. W. Norton & Co., Inc., 1966), by permission of the author.

Bateson, F. W. (pp. 112–113). Reprinted from *English Poetry* by F. W. Bateson by permission of Barnes & Noble, Inc., and Longmans, Green & Co., Ltd.

Brown, John Russell (pp. 87–88). Reprinted from *Shakespeare's Plays in Performance* by J. R. Brown by permission of St. Martin's Press, Inc., and Edward Arnold Ltd.

Coghill, Nevill (pp. 37, 38). "Wags, Clowns and Jesters," in *More Talking of Shakespeare*, edited by John Garrett (London: Longmans, Green & Co., Ltd.; and New York: Theatre Arts Books). Copyright 1959 by Longmans, Green & Co., Ltd. Reprinted by permission of Theatre Arts Books.

Drew, Elizabeth (pp. 35, 36–37). Reprinted from *The Novel: A Modern Guide to Fifteen English Masterpieces* by Elizabeth Drew. Copyright © 1963 by Elizabeth Drew and used by permission of the publisher, Dell Publishing Co., Inc.

Eliot, T. S. (p. 29). Lines from "Little Gidding" from *Four Quartets* by T. S. Eliot are reprinted by permission of Harcourt, Brace & World, Inc., and Faber and Faber, Ltd.

Fergusson, Francis (p. 82). Reprinted from *The Human Image in Dramatic Literature* by Francis Fergusson by permission of Columbia University Press. Copyright 1952, Columbia University Press.

Friedman, Norman (p. 39). Reprinted from "Point of View in Fiction," *PMLA*, LXX (1955), 1184, by permission of the Modern Language Association.

Frye, Northrop (p. 27). Reprinted from *The Well-tempered Critic* by Northrop Frye by permission of Indiana University Press.

Green, Martin (pp. 30, 59–60). Reprinted from *Re-appraisals* by Martin Green by permission of W. W. Norton & Company, Inc. Copyright © 1965, 1963 by Martin Green.

Herbert, Robert L. (pp. 4–6). Reprinted from the International Fine Arts Exhibition catalog by permission of the author and The National Gallery of Canada (Ottawa).

Joyce, James (pp. 55–56). From "Araby" from *Dubliners* by James Joyce. Originally published by B. W. Huebsch, Inc., in 1916. All rights reserved. Reprinted by permission of The Viking Press, Inc.

McCarthy, Mary (pp. 60–61). Reprinted from "Settling the Colonel's Hash" from *On the Contrary* by Mary McCarthy by permission of Farrar, Straus & Giroux, Inc.

Muir, Kenneth (p. 90). Reprinted from *Shakespeare: The Great Tragedies* (London: Longmans, Green & Co., Ltd., 1961) by Kenneth Muir by permission of the author.

Nemerov, Howard (pp. 58–59). Reprinted from *Poetry and Fiction: Essays* by Howard Nemerov by permission of Rutgers University Press.

Sewall, Richard B. (p. 39). Reprinted from *The Vision of Tragedy* by Richard B. Sewall by permission of Yale University Press.

Trilling, Lionel (pp. 27–28). From *The Liberal Imagination* by Lionel Trilling. Copyright 1940 by Lionel Trilling. Reprinted by permission of The Viking Press, Inc.

Van Ghent, Dorothy (pp. 57, 58, 68–69). Reprinted from *The English Novel* by Dorothy Van Ghent by permission of Holt, Rinehart and Winston, Inc.

PREFACE

This book is about writing, especially writing about literature. It does not attempt to cover all of the topics included in the usual rhetoric: it offers no instruction in the use of the apostrophe, no list of commonly misspelled words, no rules governing the positions of modifiers. I have assumed that these mechanical things have already been covered. What this book does offer is specific suggestions designed to help the student write effectively about literature.

The first chapter, "Writing about Literature," considers the nature of critical writing, treats matters of explication and analysis, and then discusses the problems of choosing a suitable topic and of organizing the material. The chapter concludes with a brief summary of the process of writing a critical essay.

The second chapter, "Style and Format," is a fairly short and direct approach to the elements of clear writing. It treats such matters as denotation, connotation, subordination, paragraphs, and so forth, and provides a number of specific illustrations, taken from good writers. The latter part of the chapter is devoted to the essentials of manuscript form, quotations, footnotes, and bibliography.

The third, fourth, and fifth chapters introduce the reader to various approaches used in writing about fiction, drama, and poetry. These chapters also include a number of illustrative paragraphs which should help the reader to see what good writing is and to understand the sorts of problems good writers deal with.

The sixth chapter, a brief collection of writings, contains six short essays: two on fiction, two on drama, two on poetry. Like the earlier chapters it reveals a wide range of approaches. No instructor wants his students to imitate any specific essayist, but again it is useful to have samples of adequate prose and examples of some of the things people do when they write about literature.

It is hoped that these essays, along with the earlier material on writing and documentation, will provide the student with helpful guides to writing his own readable prose and to developing his own approaches to writing about literature.

Hopefully, the preceding remarks tell the reader all that he wants to know about the scope of the book, but some further words must be added. Dr. Johnson said that "there is not so poor a book in the world that would not be a prodigious effort were it wrought out entirely by a single mind, without the aid of previous investigators." I cannot name all of the previous investigators who have helped to shape my ideas, but I must acknowledge my indebtedness to publishers and authors for permission to reprint copyrighted material, to Martin B. Friedman for several suggestions, to Morton Berman and William Burto for letting me use some passages from our *Introduction to Literature*, and to students for providing me with thousands of essays to think about. I wish also to thank those persons who offered valuable assistance by reading the manuscript, especially Richard Beal, Morton Berman, William Burto, David Giele, Albert Gilman, Eileen Mason, Ann Parker, and Warren Stone. Finally, I want to record my indebtedness to the late Hyder Edward Rollins, who was the first to show me that the commonest errors in writing about literature are easily corrected when one is alerted to look for them.

S.B.

CONTENTS

PART ONE

PART TWO

3
FICTION 53

4
DRAMA 75

5
POETRY 95

PART THREE

6
SAMPLE ESSAYS 129

A
Short Guide
to
WRITING
ABOUT LITERATURE

PART ONE

1

WRITING
ABOUT LITERATURE

THE NATURE OF
CRITICAL WRITING

In everyday talk the commonest meaning of **criticism** is something like "finding fault," and to be critical is to be censorious. But a critic can see excellences as well as faults. Because we turn to criticism with the hope that the critic has seen something we have missed, the most valuable criticism is not that which awards either medals or demerits but that which calls our attention to interesting things going on in the work of art. Here are two statements, the first by John Dryden (1631–1700), the second by W. H. Auden (1907———), suggesting that criticism is most useful when it calls our attention to things worth attending to.

They wholly mistake the nature of criticism who think its business is principally to find fault. Criticism, as it was first instituted by Aristotle, was meant a standard of judging well; the chiefest part of which is, to observe those excellencies which should delight a reasonable reader.   *Essays,* ed. W. P. Ker (Oxford, 1900), II, 225

What is the function of a critic? So far as I am concerned, he can do me one or more of the following services:

  1. Introduce me to authors or works of which I was hitherto unaware.

2. Convince me that I have undervalued an author or a work because I had not read them carefully enough.

3. Show me relations between works of different ages and cultures which I could never have seen for myself because I do not know enough and never shall.

4. Give a "reading" of a work which increases my understanding of it.

5. Throw light upon the process of artistic "Making."

6. Throw light upon the relation of art to life, to science, economics, ethics, religion, etc.

The Dyer's Hand (New York, 1963), pp. 8–9

The emphasis on observing, showing, illuminating, suggests that the function of critical writing is not very different from the commonest view of the function of imaginative writing. Here is Joseph Conrad in his preface to *The Nigger of the "Narcissus"*:

My task which I am trying to achieve is, by the power of the written word, to make you hear, to make you feel — it is, before all, to make you *see*. That — and no more, and it is everything.

Let us begin with a very brief essay, one not about literature but about painting. In *The Gleaners* Jean-François Millet presumably tried to show us certain things, and now an essayist tries to show us — tries to make us see — what Millet was doing and how he did it. The following short essay is a note in the catalog issued in conjunction with the art exhibition at the Canadian World's Fair, Expo 67.

JEAN-FRANÇOIS MILLET. 1814–1875

The Gleaners. c. 1857

Jean-François Millet, born of well-to-do Norman peasants, began his artistic training in Cherbourg. In 1837 he moved to Paris where he lived until 1849, except for a few extended visits to Normandy. With the sounds of the Revolution of 1848 still rumbling, he moved to Barbizon on the edge of the Forest of Fontainebleau, already noted as a resort of landscape painters, and there he spent the rest of his life. One of the major painters of what came to be called the Barbizon School, Millet began to celebrate the labours of the peasant, granting him a heroic dignity which expressed the aspirations of 1848. Millet's identification with the new social ideals was a result not of overtly radical views, but of his instinctive humanitarianism and his rediscovery in actual peasant life of the eternal rural world of the Bible and of Virgil, his favourite reading since youth. By

Oil. 32⅞ × 43¾ in. Musée du Louvre, Paris.

elevating to a new prominence the life of the common people, the revolutionary era released the stimulus which enabled him to continue this essential pursuit of his art and of his life.

The Gleaners, exhibited in the Salon of 1857, presents the very poorest of the peasants who are fated to bend their backs to gather with clubbed fingers the wisps of overlooked grain. That they seem so entirely wedded to the soil results from the perfect harmony of Millet's fatalistic view of man with the images which he created by a careful disposition of lines, colours and shapes. The three women are alone in the bronzed stubble of the foreground, far removed from the bustling activity of the harvesters in the distance, the riches of whose labours have left behind a few gleanings. Millet has weighted his figures ponderously downward, the busy harvest scene is literally above them, and the high horizon line which the taller woman's cap just touches emphasizes their earth-bound role suggesting that the sky is a barrier which presses down upon them, and not a source of release.

The humility of primeval labour is shown, too, in the creation of primitive archetypes rather than of individuals. Introspection such as that seen in Velazquez' *Water Carrier of Seville*, in which the three men are distinct individuals, is denied by suppressing the gleaners' features, and where the precise, fingered gestures of La Tour's *Saint*

Jerome bring his intellectual work toward his sensate mind, Millet
gives his women club-like hands which reach away from their bent
bodies toward the earth.

It was, paradoxically, the urban-industrial revolution in the nineteenth century which prompted a return to images of the pre-indus-
trial, ageless labours of man. For all their differences, both Degas and
Van Gogh were to share these concerns later, and even Gauguin was
to find in the fishermen of the South Seas that humble being, un-
tainted by the modern city, who is given such memorable form in
Millet's *Gleaners*.

Robert L. Herbert

In this essay there is, of course, evaluation or judgment as well
as interpretation or understanding. First of all, the writer assumes
it is worth his effort to talk about Millet's picture. Secondly, he
explicitly praises some qualities ("perfect harmony," "memorable
form"), but mostly the evaluation is implicit in and subordinate
to the description of what the writer sees. He sees things and calls
them to our attention as worthy of note. He points out the earth-
bound nature of the women, the difference between their hands
and those of Saint Jerome (in another picture that was in the
exhibition), the evocation of the Bible and of Virgil, etc. It is
clear that he values the picture, and he has tried to suggest some
of the reasons he values it; but he has not worried about whether
Millet is a better artist than Velazquez, or whether this is Millet's
best painting. He is content to help us see what is going on in
the picture.

Let us look for yet another moment at the **organization** or plan
of this essay. In his effort to help us see what is going on, the
author keeps his eye on his subject. His opening paragraph includes a few details (e.g., the fact that Millet was trained in
Cherbourg) that are not strictly relevant to his main point (the
vision embodied in the picture), but these must be included
because the essay is not only a critical analysis of the picture but
an informative headnote in a catalog of an exhibition of works
by more than a hundred artists. Even in this preliminary paragraph he moves quickly to the details closely related to the main
business: Millet's peasant origin, his early association with landscape painters, his humanitarianism, and his reading of the Bible
and Virgil. The second paragraph takes a close look at some
aspects of the picture (the women's hands, their position in the
foreground, the harvesters above and behind them, the oppressive
sky), and the third paragraph makes illuminating comparisons

with two other paintings. The last paragraph, like most good con-cluding paragraphs, while recapitulating the main point (the depiction of ageless labors), enlarges the vision by including references to Millet's younger contemporaries who shared his vision. Notice that this new material does not leave us looking forward to another paragraph but neatly opens up, or enriches, the matter and then turns it back to Millet. (For additional remarks on introductory and concluding paragraphs, see pp. 37–39.)

A work of literature, like a painting, is a work of art. It is an object that embodies thoughts and feelings, and study of it can increase our understanding of exactly what it is. There is an enormous body of literature worth our study, and there is a wide range of kinds of literary study designed to bring us into a closer relation with the work. Any writing that helps a reader to under-stand a literary work can properly be called literary criticism. Sometimes the critic will study the author's sources, seeking to show us — say, by a comparison between Plutarch's *Lives* and Shakespeare's *Julius Caesar* — some of the special qualities in the literary work. Sometimes he will study the author's biography, seeking to show us, for example, that Tennessee Williams' *The Glass Menagerie* draws heavily upon his childhood experiences. Sometimes he will study the anthropological and sociological background of the work, seeking to show us that a Greek tragedy owes its form to earlier rituals, or that *A Midsummer Night's Dream* is indebted to May Day customs, or that the word "thou" in Shakespeare's sonnets has a very different force from the word "you." But undergraduates are not ordinarily expected to have either the time or the familiarity with little-known material to do much in these directions except perhaps the first — source study. Usually undergraduates are being prepared to exert a trained intelligence in explicating (literally, unfolding, spreading out) or in analyzing (literally, separating into parts in order to under-stand functions and relationships) a work or a part of a work.

TWO COMMON APPROACHES: EXPLICATION AND ANALYSIS

Explication is ordinarily a line-by-line or episode-by-episode commentary on what is going on. (It takes some skill to work one's way along without saying "In line one . . . , in the second line . . . , in the third line . . . ." One must sometimes manfully say something like "The next stanza begins with . . . and then introduces . . . ." And, of course, one can discuss the second line before the first line if that seems to be the best way of handling the passage.) An explication is not a paraphrase, a rewording — though it may include paraphrase — but a commentary revealing the meaning of the work. To this end it calls attention, as it proceeds, to the connotations of words, the function of rhymes, the shifts in point of view, the development of contrasts, and any other contributions to the meaning. Take, for example, the first five lines of Milton's "Lycidas." (The subtitle is "The Author Bewails a Learned Friend, Unfortunately Drowned.")

> Yet once more, O ye laurels, and once more
> Ye myrtles brown, with ivy never sere,°   *withered*
> I come to pluck your berries harsh and crude,
> And with forced fingers rude,
> Shatter your leaves before the mellowing year.

One student's explication runs thus:

> The poem begins by insisting both on the sad occasion and on the poet's youth: the poet says that he must disturb the evergreens to pluck the "crude" berries ("crude" is used in the somewhat uncommon sense of "unripe," "immature") "before the mellowing year." The immaturity of the berries corresponds to the immaturity of the poet; he too has not yet reached the mellowing year that is necessary before he can produce a great poem, a poem of such quality that his contemporaries will deem it immortal, worthy of a crown of evergreen leaves traditionally awarded to a great poet. His fingers are "rude" in two senses: they disturb the unripe berries, and they are still untutored.
>
> The heavy stresses on the first three words ("Yet once more") help to suggest the oppressiveness of the task. The remainder of the first line and all of the second introduce a sensuousness that momentarily relieves; but "harsh and crude" in the next line returns us to the unpleasantness of the task; and the short fourth line, with its emphasis heightened by the alliteration in "forced fingers" and by the rhyme of "crude" with "rude" in the previous line (this is the first rhyme we encounter in the poem), lends a note of finality, although the grammatical sense is not completed until the fifth line. In this fifth line "leaves" is tied to "mellowing" both by meaning and by the repetition of "l"; yet we are left not with a sense of mellowing but with the fact, as the poem states, that the leaves have *not* reached the mellowing year: they are being "shattered."

An explicator who did more homework might be able to tell us that laurel, the symbol of poetry, grew on Mount Parnassus; that myrtle symbolizes undying love; and that ivy was sacred to Bacchus; but it is perhaps enough for a start to know that they are evergreens and that they are classical symbols associated with poetry.

Although the two sample paragraphs of an explication of "Lycidas" do not proceed mechanically line by line, the explication as a whole would move through the poem from beginning to end. A difficulty, of course, is that any given line or episode may take on additional meanings by virtue of what comes later. For example, the first five lines are related to lines 78–82, in which Milton says:

Fame is no plant that grows on mortal soil, . . .
But lives and spreads aloft by those pure eyes,
And perfect witness of all-judging Jove.

When he reaches lines 78–82, the explicator will probably wish to remind his readers of the contrast between this immortal plant and the evergreens (that mortals give to mortals) of the opening lines.

Because the language of a literary work is denser (richer in associations or connotations) than the language of discursive prose such as this paragraph, explication is much concerned with bringing to the surface the meanings that are in the words but that may not be immediately apparent. Explication, in short, seeks to make explicit the implicit. Sample explications, or fragments of explications, appear in Chapters 3, 4, and 5.

Analysis, a breaking of the work into parts, or the study of one or more parts, is more common than explication in the study of works longer than a page or two; though, of course, if one has world enough and time, one can set out to explicate all of *Moby-Dick* or *Paradise Lost*. (More likely, one will explicate a page in *Moby-Dick*, or a verse paragraph in *Paradise Lost*.) An analysis may, for example, consider only the functions of the setting in *The Adventures of Huckleberry Finn* or of the narrator's voice in *Paradise Lost*. Although Chapters 3 and 4 contain numerous specimens of analytic criticism, and Chapter 5 contains an analysis of the structure of one of Wordsworth's short poems, a sample analysis may be useful here.

Suppose one wants to write about the role of the clown in *Othello*. After thinking about the play and consulting the jottings made while thinking and rereading, one decides that the essay's underlying argument, or thesis — the clown *has* a role — breaks down into, say, six parts or paragraphs. (Of course, it takes a good deal of thinking and revising one's thoughts before one sees that the notes can be reasonably arranged into these groups.) The topic ideas — the ideas that will be developed in a series of paragraphs — might be these:

1. The role of the clown in *Othello* is small but significant.

2. His first appearance, with musicians beneath Othello's window in III.i, is moderately funny on the surface.

3. This scene is more than funny; it provides relief, and yet it is related to the tragic motif.

4. In his second appearance, in III.iv, he puns on the word "lie," a word central to the play.

5. The study of a relatively small detail can suggest the complexity of what goes on in Shakespeare's plays.

When properly amplified (*not* padded, but set forth with convincing detail), the essay might run thus:

The Clown in *Othello*

Of the several dozen characters in *Othello*, the clown is among the least notable. He appears in only two scenes, speaking only about thirty lines. Nothing really depends upon him. If he is cut out, Iago will still succeed in duping Othello into murdering Desdemona, and Othello will still commit suicide in the fifth act. Yet the clown is in the play, and he presumably pulls his weight.

He first appears in III.i, bandying words with the musicians whom Cassio has brought to play beneath Othello's window. Like most of Shakespeare's other clowns, this one engages in bawdy repartee. Although a modern audience does not understand the jokes until they are explained in footnotes, and then does not find them funny, presumably the Elizabethan audience understood and enjoyed the jokes and was grateful for the humor. The joke about wind instruments — "And thereby hangs a tale" — with its pun on "tail" is given the most space, leading to the paradox about "music that may not be heard."[1] But even if we assume that the scene was once funny, we may still wonder what it is doing in the play.

It does quite a bit. First, it provides relief from the preceding tension: Cassio has been deprived of his office, and Iago's plot to use Cassio as a means to destroy Othello is well under way. A few lines after the clown's scene, Cassio will raise the tension again by un-

[1] Lines 6–15. All quotations from *Othello* are taken from the Signet Classic Edition, ed. Alvin Kernan (New York, 1963).

wittingly furthering Iago's plot. But the comic business is not mere relief; it contains the metaphor of music that was introduced when Othello had good-humoredly hoped (II.i.196) that the kisses he shared with Desdemona would be their greatest discords. In an aside (II.i.198–99) Iago had said, "O, you are well tuned now! / But I'll set down the pegs that make this music"; that is, he had vowed to loosen the strings (the lovers are conceived of as two stringed instruments in harmony) in order to produce discord or disharmony. We earlier saw him introduce discord into Brabantio's house when he shouted bawdy warnings and more recently when he caused the "dreadful bell" to sound the alarm. Now, in the scene with the clown, we hear music spoken of in bawdy terms in line 19 ("put up your pipes in your bag"). The bawdiness is underlined by "for love's sake" (line 13), ordinarily an expression roughly equivalent merely to "for goodness' sake," but here with a second sexual meaning: this pipe music is banished "for love's sake" because it would interrupt the consummation of Othello's and Desdemona's marriage. Finally, in this scene there is yet another connection between the clown's jests and the tragic plot. When Cassio says, "Dost thou hear me, mine honest friend?" the clown punningly replies, "No. I hear not your honest friend. I hear you" (line 21). "Honest friend" looks back to Cassio, who has proved to be an unreliable friend and whose attempt now to regain Othello's friendship through the musicians is less than honest. Moreover, "honest friend" looks ahead to III.iii, when Iago will villainously play the role of honest friend.

The clown's second and last appearance, at the beginning of III.iv, follows the terrifying scene in which Iago, feigning to be Othello's friend, poisons Othello's mind and rouses him to murderous thoughts. Again the clown provides relief by his punning, and again the punning is relevant to the tragic plot. Desdemona asks him (line 1) where "Cassio lies" — that is, where Cassio lives or lodges — and the clown pretends to take the word in the sense of "tells untruths": "I dare not say he lies anywhere. . . . He's a soldier, and for me to say a soldier lies, 'tis stabbing" (lines 3–6). "Lie" and "lies" are mentioned seven times in this brief encounter which is the prelude to a series of tragic lies later in the scene: Emilia lies when she says she does not know where Desdemona's handkerchief is; Othello lies when he says he is untroubled; Desdemona lies when she says she has not lost the handkerchief. Iago, of course, has already lied and will continue to lie. No less important, the clown's insistent use of "lie" is the prelude to the appearance of the word in the next scene, when (IV.i.36–37) Othello bitterly puns on the sexual meaning: "Lie with her? Lie on her? — We say lie on her when they belie her. Lie with her!" Desdemona, of course, has been belied; she and Cassio did not lie together.

We need not worry about whether or not Shakespeare was conscious of the threads that tie the clown to the tragic plot. Possibly he was not; possibly his mind unconsciously introduced the bawdy references to music after the figure of Othello and Desdemona as "well tuned." Possibly, too, the clown's puns on "lie" were thought to be no more than jokes to provide a light moment between scenes of great tension. But these jokes do in fact connect with other things in the play, making their contribution, however small, to the tragedy of *Othello*. It is not surprising that in *Othello*, as in any other work of genius, a complexity of artistry and a subtlety of meaning pervade even the smallest details.

Although Chapter 2 will offer some detailed suggestions about writing, we can pause a moment here to call attention to several principles.

1. The introductory paragraph, with its reference to all of the characters, begins with a relatively wide view and then moves in on its subject, the clown. By the end of the paragraph the exact topic — "What does the clown do?" — is introduced.

2. The next four paragraphs, the body of the essay, discuss the clown's role in his two scenes; his first appearance is, reasonably, considered first.

3. Some brief and relevant quotations are used. They give the reader the necessary details, and they do not interrupt the flow of the argument as long quotations are likely to do.

4. The writer assumes that the reader has read the work being discussed; therefore, he does not fill his essay with a tedious synopsis. But aware that the reader has not memorized the work, the writer gives him helpful reminders, as in "He first appears in III.i, bandying words with the musicians whom Cassio has brought . . . ."

5. The writer has opinions, but he keeps himself in the background, for the most part revealing the work rather than himself.

6. The present tense is used in narrating the action of a play or a piece of fiction, as in "He first appears in III.i . . . ," and in "When Cassio says . . . ." Of course, earlier actions will require a past tense, later actions the future, but in narrating what *is* happening use the present.

7. The concluding paragraph has a structure more or less the reverse of the introductory paragraph. It moves from the clown in *Othello* to art in general, setting the particular topic in a framework.

Only points 2 and 4 can be thought of as rules: an essay must be organized and must not synopsize unnecessarily. The other points are not rules but rather are time-tested procedures that may be of help.

FINDING A
MANAGEABLE TOPIC

1. If a topic is assigned, write on it.

2. If you are to choose a topic, choose one that can be treated thoroughly within the allotted space. Unless you have an enormous amount of time for reflection and revision, you cannot write a meaningful essay of five hundred or even a thousand words on "Character in *Hamlet*" or on "Figurative Language in *Othello*" or on "Symbolism in *Moby-Dick*." If you have read the work thoughtfully, you ought to be able to find a much smaller topic, one that you can think hard about for the relatively few hours that you have, and that you can discuss in detail within the limits of the paper. Do not try to say everything you know about the work; choose a compassable topic and stay with it throughout your essay. A "smaller" topic need not be a dull or trivial topic; treated properly, it may illuminate the entire work, or, to change the metaphor, it may serve as a mine-shaft that gives entry to the work. "Hamlet's Relationship to Horatio," properly studied, will in five hundred or a thousand words tell a reader more (and will have taught its author more) than will "Hamlet as a Tragic Hero." Similarly, "Huck Finn's Imagination" is a better topic than "The Character of Huck Finn," and "The Meanings of 'Economy' in *Walden*" a better topic than "The Meaning of *Walden*."

How do you find a topic? An idea may hit you suddenly; as you are reading you find yourself jotting in the margin, "Contrast with Joyce's treatment of disillusionment," or "too heavy irony." Or an idea may come slowly on rereading. Perhaps you gradually become aware of the frequency of "really" in *The Catcher in the Rye*, and you notice that Holden Caulfield, who is regularly given to saying things like "if you really want to know" and "I really mean it," at one point explicitly comments on the nature of reality. You work on this and begin to relate it to his abundant discussions of phoneys, and you emerge, perhaps, with the **thesis**, or argument, or proposition, that in Holden's mouth "really" is not merely the filler it seems to be but is a clue to his quest for the real in a world of appearances or phoneys. If you have thought about the topic, converted it into a thesis, and stripped it of irrelevancies, you should be able to formulate it in a few words. This formula, or something like it, is your title. There is nothing wrong with a title as direct as "Holden's Use of 'Really' "; although it is scarcely exciting, it is informative. Beware of cute titles, especially those that do not give the reader a good idea of what will follow such as "Really" or "A Boy's Word." "The Real Holden and Reality" is about as far as one can go. One other example of a thesis may be useful here: Mark Van Doren's analysis of Wordsworth's "The Solitary Reaper" is held together by his proposition (p. 154) that the poem is admirable "yet each stanza is inferior to the one before it." Van Doren does not simply talk at random about the poem; he has an argument and he presents it.

Every literary work affords its own topics, and every essayist must set forth his own thesis, but a few useful generalizations may be made. You can often find a thesis by asking one of two questions:

1. What is this doing? That is, why is this scene in the novel or play? Why is the clown in *Othello*? Why are these lines unrhymed? Why is this stanza form employed?

2. How was this done? That is, how did the author make this character funny or dignified or pathetic? How did he communicate the idea that this character is a bore without boring me? Why do I find this poem witty?

The chapters on fiction, drama, and poetry try to provide the relevant critical vocabulary; they also try to do two other things: suggest the sorts of problems critics write about, and offer paragraphs that can serve as models of critical writing. After reading the chapter on fiction, for example, one should have not only some idea of what plot, symbolism, setting, etc., are but also some idea of how to write about them. It is primarily from those chapters and from your instructor that you should get a sense of what are appropriate topics, but a few examples are offered here. For the sake of clarity, these topics are stated baldly. They are rough beginnings and need to be shaped into theses. Consider the difference between "Hamlet's Relationship to Horatio" (an unshaped topic) and the thesis it might yield: Although Hamlet

admires Horatio's stoic temperament and values his companion-
ship, Hamlet has the greater temperament of a hero.

Sample Topics in Fiction

PLOT
>"Death as a Device to Link Episodes in *Huckleberry Finn*"
>"The Appropriateness of the Ending of *Lord of the Flies*"

THEME
>"Absurdity in Camus' *The Plague*"
>"Paralysis in Joyce's *Dubliners*"
>"Imagery as a Revelation of Theme in . . ."

CHARACTER (Sometimes a mere character sketch may be acceptable; more often one will study character to see how it contributes
to the theme or how it helps to define another character.)
>"What Holden Caulfield is *Really* Like"
>"Stephen Dedalus: Prig or Artist?"
>"The Function of the Three Mates in *Moby-Dick*"
>"The Distinctive Language of Huck Finn"

FORESHADOWING (Really an aspect of Plot and Character)
>"Suspense and Surprise in . . ."
>"Early Tragic Overtones in *Moby-Dick*"
>"The Humor of the Unexpected"

SETTING
>"The Function of the Setting in . . ."
>"Contrasts in the Settings in . . ."

SYMBOLISM
>"The Meaning of the White Whale"
>"Walls in *Bartleby*"
>"The River in *Huckleberry Finn*"
>"The Sun in Camus' *The Stranger*"

POINT OF VIEW
>"Objectivity in 'The Killers' "
>"Editorializing in *Tess of the D'Urbervilles*"
>"The Unreliable Narrator in . . ."

Sample Topics in Drama

In addition to topics similar to those above on theme, character,
foreshadowing, setting, and symbolism, the following topics may
be useful examples.

IRONY

"Unconscious Irony in *Macbeth*"

"Conscious Irony in *Major Barbara*"

TRAGEDY

"King Oedipus: Tragic Hero or Pathetic Victim?"

"A Comparison between King Oedipus and Willy Loman"

"Willy Loman and Arthur Miller's Theory of Tragedy"

"Sartre's *No Exit*: A Tragedy without a Tragic Hero"

COMEDY

"The Comic in the Tragic: Beckett's *Waiting for Godot*"

"The Two Jesters in *As You Like It*"

"The Comic Portrayal of Villainy in . . ."

"Tragic Implications in *Major Barbara*"

PLOT

"The Relevance of the Subplot in *King Lear*"

"Coincidence in *Ghosts*"

"The Turning Point in . . ."

"Flashbacks in *Death of a Salesman*"

GESTURES

"Comic Mannerisms in . . ."

"Appropriate Gestures for Hamlet in the Prayer Scene"

Sample Topics in Poetry

VOICE

"The Character of the Duke in 'My Last Duchess' "

"The New England Voice in Frost's Poems"

"Prufrock's Self-irony"

DICTION

"The Use of Colloquialisms in Frost"

"Shifts in Diction in Allen Ginsberg"

FIGURATIVE LANGUAGE

"Scientific Imagery in a Poem by Donne"

"Metaphors of the Theater in Yeats's 'Lapis Lazuli' "

"Organic Metaphors in a Poem by Whitman"

SYMBOLISM

"Frost's Woods and Stars"

"The City in Robert Lowell's Poetry"

STRUCTURE
    "Logic and Illogic in . . ."
    "Paradox in . . ."

IRONY
    "Understatement in . . ."

PATTERNS OF SOUND
    "Rhyme and Reason in . . ."
    "The Significance of Metrical Variations in . . ."
    "The Not-So-Free Verse of 'When Lilacs Last in the Door-
    yard Bloom'd' "

CONSIDERING
THE EVIDENCE

Once you have your topic ("The Clown in *Othello*") and have
shaped it into a thesis ("The clown is relevant"), be certain that
you have all the evidence. Usually this means that you should
study the context of the material you are discussing. An excerpt
from A. E. Housman serves as a famous instance of the failure
to keep the context in mind. Housman wrote of a line in Milton's
Arcades:

> But in these six simple words of Milton —
>
>   Nymphs and shepherds, dance no more —
>
> what is it that can draw tears, as I know it can, to the eyes of more
> readers than one? What in the world is there to cry about? Why
> have the mere words the physical effect of pathos when the sense of
> the passage is blithe and gay? I can only say, because they are poetry,
> and find their way to something in man which is obscure and latent,
> something older than the present organization of his nature.
>
>   *The Name and Nature of Poetry* (New York, 1933), p. 45

This tells us something about Housman but nothing about the
line in *Arcades*; in its context the line is not a command to stop
dancing but only to stop dancing "By sandy Ladon's lillied banks"
and to come to "A better soil."

Similarly, if, for example, you are talking about images of light
and dark, take account of *all* of the images of this sort. Some
may not fit the pattern you discern in the vast majority, but fair-
ness and self-protection require that you call attention to the
exceptions and indicate why they do not destroy your thesis.

Before you argue that because Holden distrusts the adult world, "old" is his ultimate word of condemnation, remember that he speaks of "old Phoebe" and of "old Thomas Hardy," both of whom he values highly. Before you argue that the style of *Romeo and Juliet* is highly formal, remember that it includes such lines as "Where's Potpan, that he helps not to take away? He shift a trencher! He scrape a trencher!" (There *is* a good deal of highly formal writing in the play, and an essay can be written on it, but the essayist should be aware that it has other styles too.) Before you argue that the imagery in *Romeo and Juliet* associates the lovers with light and death with dark, remember that not every image of light and dark works this way. At the beginning of the play several extended passages associate the infatuated Romeo with darkness. The discrepancy can be explained; it must be explained.

Two additional relevant concerns: 1) know what the words mean, and 2) know the limitations of the reprint you are using. The first point is obvious. Pay attention to footnotes if they are given; look up words and allusions that are obscure to you, and, if the piece is not recent, consider the possibility that a word that looks familiar but that makes little sense may have an older and different meaning. When Pope says that he will "catch the manners living as they rise," "manners" denotes not etiquette but kinds or psychological types, an obsolete usage except in such a phrase as "What manner of man is he?" The second point, the limitations of your text, may or may not be relevant, depending on the nature of the assignment. If the instructor tells you to stay with the page in front of you, work from that. But if you are given more freedom, you may find it advisable to know something about the reprint you are working from. Some editors provide a "Note on the Text," telling you whether they are reprinting the first or the last edition, listing their emendations, etc. By reading the editor's textual note you may learn, for example, that although he has printed the first two lines of Shakespeare's "Sonnet 146" thus:

Poor soul, the center of my sinful earth,
Thrall to these rebel pow'rs that thee array,

the only authoritative text (1609) — the text from which all other texts are derived — did not print "Thrall to," but accidentally reprinted "my sinful earth." "Thrall to" is merely an editor's guess; among other guesses are "Fooled by," "Leagued with," and "Rebuke." Any other two syllables that will make sense are equally valid guesses. Clearly it is unwise to build an interpretation that rests heavily on any of these guesses. A final example illustrates the point: Henry James revised his novels for the New York Edition; therefore, before you talk about his development from the early novels to the late ones, make sure that you have read the early novels and not late revisions of them.

ORGANIZING
THE MATERIAL

After locating a topic, converting it into a thesis, and weighing the evidence, the writer has the job of organizing the material into a coherent whole, a series of paragraphs that steadily builds up an effective argument. Notice, for example, that the paragraphs in the essay on *Othello* (pp. 10–12) cannot be shuffled about without a loss in clarity. The idea of discussing the earlier scene before the later scene is reasonable; and, indeed, if the discussion of the two scenes were reversed, the writer would have to have a good reason for violating the play's chronology. He might have such a reason. If, for instance, he felt that the second scene was much slighter, he might take it up first, explaining that it is best to get this less important scene out of the way before turning to the heart of the matter, the clown's first scene. Such an arrangement would avoid an anticlimax that might cause the reader to lose interest after the midpoint. Again, to avoid an anticlimax, the writer might reverse the chronological order if there were evidence in the work that ran counter to his thesis — but had to be shown — and this evidence came chronologically after the evidence supporting his thesis. As another illustration of the way in which a writer arranges his paragraphs meaningfully and signals the arrangement to the reader, consider these opening words from nine consecutive paragraphs in Richard Fogle's *Hawthorne's Fiction*: "In the same chapter. . . ." "From this scene onward. . . ." "From the victim's point of view. . . ." "Along with this steady irony. . . ." "The character of Pearl illuminates this point. . . ." "These qualities of concentration, selectivity, and irony. . . ." "Thus the imagery of hell-fire. . . ." "Puritan demonology is in general. . . ." "This use of the past. . . ."

Something should be said about an essay organized around a

comparison or a contrast, say, between the settings in two novels or between two characters in a novel or between the symbolism in two poems. Probably the student's first thought, after making some jottings, is to discuss one half of the comparison and then to go on to the second half. Instructors and textbooks usually condemn such an organization, arguing that the essay breaks into two parts, and that the second part involves a good deal of repetition of categories set up in the first part. Usually they recommend that the student organize his thoughts differently, somewhat along these lines:

1. First similarity
   a. first work (or character, or characteristic)
   b. second work
2. Second similarity
   a. first work
   b. second work
3. First difference
   a. first work
   b. second work
4. Second difference
   a. first work
   b. second work

and so on, for as many additional differences as seem relevant. For example, if one wishes to compare *Huckleberry Finn* with *The Catcher in the Rye,* one may organize the material thus:

1. First similarity (the narrator and his quest)
   a. Huck
   b. Holden
2. Second similarity (the corrupt world surrounding the narrator)
   a. society in *Huckleberry Finn*
   b. society in *The Catcher*
3. First difference (degree to which the narrator fulfills his quest and escapes from society)
   a. Huck's plan to "light out" to the frontier
   b. Holden's breakdown

Here is another way of organizing a comparison and contrast:

1. First point: the narrator and his quest
   a. similarities between Huck and Holden
   b. differences between Huck and Holden

   2. Second point: the corrupt world
     a. similarities between the worlds in *Huck* and *The Catcher*
     b. differences in the worlds in *Huck* and *The Catcher*
   3. Third point: degree of success
     a. similarities between Huck and Holden
     b. differences between Huck and Holden

But a comparison need not employ either of these structures. There is even the danger that an essay employing either of them may not come into focus until the essayist stands back from his seven-layer cake and announces, in his concluding paragraph, that the odd layers taste better. In one's preparatory thinking, one may want to make comparisons in pairs (Good-natured humor: the clown in *Othello*, the clownish grave-digger in *Hamlet*; Social satire: the clown in *Othello*, the grave-digger in *Hamlet*; Relevance to main theme: . . . ; Length of role: . . . ; Comments by other characters: . . .), but one must come to some conclusions about what these add up to before writing the final version, and this final version should not duplicate the thought processes. Rather, it should be organized so as to make the point clearly and effectively. After reflection, for example, one may believe that although there are superficial similarities between the clown in *Othello* and the clownish grave-digger in *Hamlet*, there are essential differences; then in the finished essay one probably will not wish to obscure the main point by jumping back and forth from play to play, working through a series of similarities and differences. It may be better to discuss the clown in *Othello* and then to point out that, although the grave-digger in *Hamlet* resembles him in A, B, and C, the grave-digger also has other functions (D, E, and F) and is of greater consequence to *Hamlet* than the clown is to *Othello*. There will be some repetition in the second half of the essay (e.g., "The grave-digger's puns come even faster than the clown's. . . ."), but the repetition will serve to bind the two halves into a meaningful whole, making clear the degree of similarity or difference. The point of the essay presumably is not to list pairs of similarities or differences, but to illuminate a work, or works, by making thoughtful comparisons. In a long essay one cannot postpone until p. 30 a discussion of the other half of the comparison, but in an essay of, say, less than ten pages there is nothing wrong with setting forth one half of the comparison and then, in its light, the other half. The essay will break into two unrelated parts if the second half makes no use of the first, or if it does not modify the first half, but not if the second half looks back to the first half and calls attention to differences that the new material reveals. A student ought to learn how to write an essay with interwoven comparisons, but he ought also to know that there is another way to write a comparison.

The point of a comparison is to call attention to the unique features of something by holding it up against something similar but significantly different. If the differences are great and apparent, a comparison is a waste of effort. ("Blueberries are different from elephants. Blueberries do not have trunks. And elephants do not grow on bushes.") Indeed, a comparison between essentially and evidently unlike things can only obscure, for by making the comparison the writer implies there are significant similarities, and the reader can only wonder why he does not see them. The essays that do break into two halves are essays that make uninstructive comparisons: the first half tells us about five qualities in Dickens, the second half tells us about five different qualities in Dylan Thomas.

COMMUNICATING
JUDGMENTS

Because a critical essay is a judicious attempt to see what is going on in a work, or in a part of a work, the voice of the explicator or analyst sounds, on first hearing, impartial; but good explication and good analysis include — at least implicitly — evaluation. The critic may say not only that the setting changes (a neutral expression) but also that "the novelist aptly shifts the setting" or "unconvincingly describes . . ." or "effectively juxtaposes. . . ." These evaluations he supports with evidence. The critic has feelings about the work under discussion, and he reveals them, not by continually saying "I feel" and "this moves me," but by calling attention to the degree of success or failure he perceives.

One final remark on communicating judgments: write sincerely. Sincerity alone will not get an A, for it must be united with intelligence, diligence, and clarity of expression. But any attempt to neglect your own thoughtful responses and replace them with fabrications designed to please an instructor will surely fail. It is hard enough to find the words that clearly communicate your responses; it is impossible to find the words that express your hunch about what your instructor expects your responses to be.

A REVIEW:
HOW TO WRITE
AN EFFECTIVE ESSAY

Everyone must work out his own procedures and rituals, but the following suggestions may provide some help.

1. Read the work carefully.

2. Choose a worthwhile and compassable subject, something you think merits your time and is not so big that your handling of it must be superficial. As you work, give shape to your topic, narrowing it, for example, from "The Character of Hester Prynne" to "The Effects of Alienation on Hester Prynne."

3. Reread the work, taking notes (preferably on 3 x 5 cards, writing on one side only) of all relevant matters. As you read, reflect on your reading and record your reflections. If you have an idea, jot it down; don't assume that you will remember it when you get around to writing your essay.

4. Sort out your cards into some kind of reasonable divisions, and reject cards irrelevant to your topic. As you work you may decide that there is a better way of grouping your notes. If so, start reorganizing. If you are writing an explication, the order probably is essentially the order of the lines or of the episodes, but if you are writing an analysis you may wish to organize your essay from the lesser material to the greater (to avoid anticlimax) or from the simple to the complex (to insure intelligibility). If, for example, you are discussing the roles of three characters in a story, it may be best to build up to the one of the three that you think the most important. If you are comparing two characters, it may be best to move from the most obvious contrasts to the least obvious. When you have arranged your notes into a meaningful sequence of packets, you have approximately divided your material into paragraphs.

5. Jot down an outline, indicating the topic idea of each paragraph, and under each topic idea jot down the supporting details that give it substance. (Suggestions for introductory and concluding paragraphs are given on pp. 37–39.)

6. Reread the work, looking for additional material that strengthens or weakens your main point; take account of it in your notes and in your outline.

7. With your outline in front of you, write a draft, thoughtfully checking your notes for fuller details, such as supporting

quotations. If, as you work, you find that some points in your outline are no longer relevant, eliminate them; but make sure that the argument flows from one point to the next.

8. After a suitable interval, preferably a few days, read the draft with a view toward revising it, not with a view toward congratulating yourself. As you read, correct infelicities of style (e.g., awkward repetitions, inflated or vulgar language, faulty parallels), add supporting detail where the argument is undeveloped (a paragraph of only one or two sentences is usually an undeveloped paragraph), and ruthlessly delete irrelevancies however interesting and well written they may be. But remember that a deletion probably requires some adjustment in the preceding and subsequent material. Make sure that the argument, aided by transitions, runs smoothly. The details should be relevant, the organization reasonable, the argument clear. Check all quotations for accuracy. If there is time, put the revision aside, thoughtfully reread it in a day or two, and revise it again.

9. Type a clean copy, following the principles (concerning margins, pagination, footnotes, etc.) set forth in the next chapter. If you have borrowed any ideas, be sure to give credit (usually in footnotes) to your sources. Remember that plagiarism is not limited to the unacknowledged borrowing of words; a borrowed idea, even when put into your own words, requires acknowledgment.

10. Proofread and neatly make corrections as explained on page 41.

2

STYLE AND FORMAT

SOME REMARKS
ABOUT WRITING

Writing is hard work (Lewis Carroll's school in *Alice's Adventures in Wonderland* taught reeling and writhing), and there is no point in fooling ourselves into believing that it is all a matter of inspiration. There is ample evidence that many of the poems, stories, and plays that seem (as we read them) to flow so effortlessly were in fact the product of innumerable revisions. "Hard labor for life" was Conrad's view of his career as a writer. There is no guarantee that effort will pay off, but failure to expend effort is sure to result in writing that will strike the reader as slovenly, not worth reading. If duty compels the reader to stay with it, he will read it with increasing displeasure; if it is really bad, he will be baffled as well as displeased.

Big books have been written on the elements of good writing, but the best way to learn to write is to do your best, revise it a few days later, submit it, and then study the annotations an experienced reader puts on your essay. In revising the offending passages, you will learn what your weaknesses are. After drafting your next essay, put it aside for a day or so; when you reread it, preferably aloud, you may find much that offends. If the argument does not flow, check to see whether your organization is reasonable and whether you have made adequate transitions. Do not hesitate to delete interesting but irrelevant material that obscures the argument. Make the necessary revisions and repeat the process if there is time. Revision is indispensable if you wish to avoid (in Maugham's words) "the impression of writing with the stub of a blunt pencil."

Still, a few principles can be briefly set forth here. On Dr. Johnson's belief that men do not so much need to be taught as they need to be reminded, these principles are brief imperatives rather than detailed instructions.

Get the Right Word

Denotation. Be sure the word you choose has the right denotation (explicit meaning). Don't say "tragic" when you mean "pathetic," "sarcastic" when you mean "ironic," "free verse" when you mean "blank verse," "disinterested" when you mean "uninterested."

Connotation. Be sure the word you choose has the right connotation (association, implication). Here are three examples of words with the wrong connotations for their contexts: "The heroic spirit is not dead. It still *lurks* in the hearts of men." ("Lurks" suggests a furtiveness inappropriate to the heroic spirit. Something like "lives" or "dwells" is needed.) "Close study will *expose* the strength of Wordsworth's style." ("Reveal" would be better than "expose" here; "expose" suggests that some weakness will be brought to light, as in "Close study will expose the flimsiness of the motivation.") "Although Creon suffers, his suffering is not great enough to *relegate* him to the role of tragic hero." (In place of "relegate him to," we need something like "elevate" or "exalt.")

Concreteness. Catch the richness, complexity, and uniqueness of things. Do not write "Here one sees his lack of emotion" if you really mean "Here one sees his indifference" or "his iciness" or "his impartiality" or whatever the exact condition is. *Not* "The clown's part in *Othello* is very small" but "The clown appears in only two scenes in *Othello*" or "The clown in *Othello* speaks only thirty lines." ("Very," as in "very small" or "very big," is almost never the right word. A role is rarely "very big"; it "dominates" or "overshadows" or "is second only to . . . .")

In addition to using the concrete word and the appropriate detail, use illustrative **examples**. Northrop Frye, talking about the perception of rhythm, illustrates his point:

> Ideally, our literary education should begin, not with prose, but with such things as "this little pig went to market" — with verse rhythm reinforced by physical assault. The infant who gets bounced on somebody's knee to the rhythm of "Ride a cock horse" does not need a footnote telling him that Banbury Cross is twenty miles northeast of Oxford. He does not need the information that "cross" and "horse" make (at least in the pronunciation he is most likely to hear) not a rhyme but an assonance. . . . All he needs is to get bounced.   *The Well-tempered Critic*
> (Bloomington, Indiana, 1963), p. 25

Frye does not say our literary education should begin with "simple rhymes" or with "verse popular with children." He says "with such things as 'this little pig went to market,' " and then he goes on to add "Ride a cock horse." We know exactly what he means. Notice, too, that we do not need a third example. Be detailed, but know when to stop.

Your reader is likely to be brighter and more demanding than Lady Pliant, who in a seventeenth-century play says to a would-be seducer, "You are very alluring — and say so many fine Things, and nothing is so moving to me as a fine Thing." Fine Things, of course, are what is wanted, but only exact words and apt illustrations will convince an intelligent reader that he is hearing fine things.

Levels of usage. Although the dividing lines cannot always be drawn easily, tradition recognizes three levels: formal, informal, and vulgar or popular, though sometimes "popular" is used to designate a level between informal and vulgar. **Formal writing** — at its highest or most formal — presumes considerable importance in the writer, the audience, and the topic. A noted figure, say a respected literary critic, examining an influential book and addressing the world of thoughtful readers, may use a highly formal style, as Lionel Trilling does here, in a criticism of V. L. Parrington's *Main Currents in American Literature*:

> To throw out Poe because he cannot be conveniently fitted into a theory of American culture, to speak of him as a biological sport and as a mind apart from the main current, to find his gloom to be

merely personal and eccentric, "only the atrabilious wretchedness of a dipsomaniac," as Hawthorne's was "no more than the skeptical questioning of life by a nature that knew no fierce storms," to judge Melville's response to American life to be less noble than that of Bryant or of Greeley, to speak of Henry James as an escapist, as an artist similar to Whistler, a man characteristically afraid of stress — this is not merely to be mistaken in aesthetic judgment; rather it is to examine without attention and from the point of view of a limited and essentially arrogant conception of reality the documents which are in some respects the most suggestive testimony to what America was and is, and of course to get no answer from them.

The Liberal Imagination (New York, 1950), p. 21

Consider also the beginning of the Gettysburg Address; unless you are the President of the United States dedicating a national cemetery during a civil war, it is best not to speak of "Four score and seven years." "Eighty-seven" or "nearly a hundred" will have to do. Of course, formal English includes many simple words ("four," "and," "seven"), but it is notable for its use of relatively uncommon words, such as "score" and "hallow," and its long sentences, balanced or antithetical, which suspend their meaning until the end. Notice that in Trilling's sentence the structure is this: "To throw . . . , to speak . . . , to find . . . , to judge . . . , to speak . . . ," and we still do not have an independent clause. Two-thirds of the way through, with "this is not merely to be mistaken," the previous words come into focus, but the meaning is still incomplete. To do such-and-such "is not merely to be mistaken," but what *is* it to be? At last we are told: "It is to examine without attention . . . and . . . to get no answer . . . ."

A formal sentence need not be lengthy. Here is a fairly short formal sentence by W. H. Auden: "Owing to its superior power as a mnemonic, verse is superior to prose as a medium for didactic instruction." In another frame of mind Auden might have written something less formal, along these lines: "Because it stays more easily in the memory, verse is better than prose for teaching." This revision of Auden's sentence can be called **informal,** but it is high on the scale, the language of an educated man writing courteously to an audience conceived of as his peers. It is the level of almost all serious writing about literature. A low informal version might be: "Poetry sticks in the mind better than prose; so if you want to teach something, poetry is better." This is the language any of us might use in our most casual moments; it is almost never the language used in writing about literature.

Below low informal is the **vulgar** language of near-illiterates ("Poems stays in me mind like words don't. Poems teach good"), who do not write essays on literature. People who do write essays on literature should not treat their subject and their reader as though they were members of the family with whom they might horse around. (This last sentence, already too informal by virtue of "horse around," could be made even more offensive: "They shouldn't fool around with what they're talking about and with their reader like they're horsing around with the kids.") In between high formal and vulgar English is the language educated people use when writing with some respect for their subject and for their audience. Don't be stuffy, and don't be coarse. Be serious but not solemn. There is rarely any need to write that in *Measure for Measure* Claudio is "incarcerated" or that Claudio is "thrown in the clink." "Imprisoned" will probably do the job best. Nor will it do to "finagle" with an inappropriate expression by putting it in "quotes." As the previous sentence indicates, the quotation marks do not make such expressions acceptable, only more obvious and more offensive. The quotation marks tell the reader that the writer knows he is using the wrong word but is too lazy to find the right word. If for some reason a relatively low word is the right one, use it and don't apologize with quotation marks (for instance, the use of "fiddle-faddle" without quotation marks on p. 81).

In short, in "every phrase/And sentence that is right," as T. S. Eliot says in *Four Quartets*,

> every word is at home,
> Taking its place to support the others,
> The word neither diffident nor ostentatious,
> An easy commerce of the old and the new,
> The common word exact without vulgarity,
> The formal word precise but not pedantic,
> The complete consort dancing together.

Repetition and variation. Although some repetitions — say, of words like "surely" or "it is noteworthy" — reveal a tic that ought to be cured by revision, don't be afraid to repeat a word if it is the best word. The following paragraph repeats "interesting," "paradox," "Salinger," "what makes," and "book"; note also "feel" and "feeling."

The reception given to *Franny and Zooey* in America has illustrated
again the interesting paradox of Salinger's reputation there; great
public enthusiasm, of the *Time* magazine and Best Seller List kind,
accompanied by a repressive coolness in the critical journals. What
makes this a paradox is that the book's themes are among the most
ambitiously highbrow, and its craftsmanship most uncompromisingly
virtuoso. What makes it an interesting one is that those who are
most patronising about the book are those who most resemble its
characters; people whose ideas and language in their best moments
resemble Zooey's. But they feel they ought not to enjoy the book.
There is a very strong feeling in American literary circles that
Salinger and love of Salinger must be discouraged.

> Martin Green, *Re-appraisals* (New York, 1965), p. 197

Repetition, a device necessary for continuity and clarity, holds
the paragraph together. There are, of course, variations: *"Franny
and Zooey"* becomes "the book," and then instead of "the
book's" we get "its." Similarly, "those who" becomes "people,"
which in turn becomes "they." Such substitutions, which neither
confuse nor distract, keep the paragraph from sounding like a
broken phonograph record.

Pronouns are handy substitutes, and they ought to be used,
but other substitutes need not always be sought. An ungrounded
fear of repetition often produces a vice known as **elegant variation**: having mentioned *Franny and Zooey*, an essayist next
speaks of "the previously mentioned work," then of "the tale,"
and finally of "this work of our author." This is far worse than
repetition; it strikes the reader as silly. Pointless variation of this
sort, it must be noted, is not to be confused with a variation that
communicates additional useful information, such as "these two
stories about the Glass family"; this variation is entirely legitimate, indeed necessary, for it furthers the discussion. But elegant
variation can be worse than silly; it can be confusing, as in —
to take a simple example — "My first *theme* dealt with plot, but
this *essay* deals with character." The reader wonders if the writer
means to suggest that an essay is different from a theme. Look
at another example: "*Writers* of the nineteenth century, unlike
authors of the twentieth . . . ." Of course, these examples are
obvious; but if, for instance, "writers" and "authors" had been
separated by a few sentences, the reader might be genuinely puzzled, wondering if he had missed some distinction that the
essayist had made.

Notice in these lucid sentences by Helen Gardner the repetition of "end" and "beginning."

> *Othello* has this in common with the tragedy of fortune, that the
> end in no way blots out from the imagination the glory of the
> beginning. But the end here does not merely by its darkness throw
> up into relief the brightness that was. On the contrary, beginning
> and end chime against each other. In both the value of life and love
> is affirmed.   *The Noble Moor* (Oxford, 1956), p. 203

The substitution of "conclusion" or "last scene" for the second
"end" would be pointless; indeed, it would destroy Miss Gardner's point that there is *identity* or correspondence between beginning and end.

On the other hand, do not repeat a word if it is being used
in a different sense. Get a different word. Example of the fault:
"This *theme* deals with the *theme* of the novel." (The first
"theme" means "essay"; the second means "underlying idea,"
"motif.") Another example of the fault: "Caesar's *character* is
complex. The comic *characters* too have some complexity." (The
first "character" means "personality"; the second means "persons," "figures in the play."

The sound of sense. Avoid awkward repetitions of sound, as
in "The story is marked by a remarkable mystery," "The reason
the season is April," "Circe certainly," "This is seen in the scene
in which . . . ." These irrelevant echoes call undue attention to
the words. On the other hand, wordplay can be effective when it
contributes to meaning. For example, Miss Gardner's statement
that in the beginning and the end of *Othello* "the value of life
and love is affirmed," makes effective use of the similarity in
sound between "life" and "love." Her implication is that these
two things that sound alike are indeed closely related, an idea
that reinforces her contention that the beginning and the end of
the play are in a way identical.

Write Effective Sentences

Wordiness. Say everything relevant, but say it in the fewest
words possible. Example of wordiness: "There are a few vague
parts in the story which give it a mysterious quality." Better: "A
few vague parts in the story give it a mysterious quality." (Nothing has been lost by the deletion of "There are" and "which.")
Probably even better: "A few vague parts add mystery to the
story." The original version says nothing that the second version
does not say, and says nothing that the third version — nine
words against fifteen — does not say. Another example: "Sophocles' tragic play *Antigone* is mistitled because Creon is the tragic

hero, and the play should be named for him." These twenty words can be reduced, with no loss of meaning, to nine words: "Sophocles' *Antigone* is mistitled; Creon is the tragic hero." There is something wrong with a sentence if you can delete words and not sense the loss. Examples of locutions that need trimming: "rising crescendo," "red in color," "illiterates who cannot read." But in cutting out dead wood, do not cut out supporting detail. Supporting detail is wordiness only when the details are so numerous and obvious that they offend the reader's intelligence.

Overpredication commonly is wordy. Don't write "A novel that is ill-constructed seldom pleases a reader," but rather "An ill-constructed novel seldom pleases a reader." Beware especially of "that . . . that," as in "A novel that is ill-constructed seldom pleases a public that is discerning." Better: "An ill-constructed novel seldom pleases a discerning public." A writer has a piece of information he wishes to convey. Does it deserve a word, a phrase, or a clause? If he has written "A novel that is ill-constructed seldom pleases a public that is discerning," he ought on rereading to see that he has given two clauses to material that can be said in two words.

The **passive voice** (the subject is the object of the action) is a common source of wordiness. Do not say "This story was written by Melville"; better: "Melville wrote this story." The revision is one-third shorter, and it says everything that the longer version says. Sometimes, of course, the passive voice, although less vigorous, may be preferable to the active voice. Example: "The novel was received in silence." To say "Readers neglected the novel" is to make the readers' response more active than it was. The passive catches the passivity of the response. Furthermore, the revision makes "Readers" the subject, but the true subject is (as in the original) the novel.

Parallels. Use parallels to clarify relationships. Few of us are likely to compose such deathless parallels as "I came, I saw, I conquered," or "of the people, by the people, for the people," but we can see to it that in our writing coordinate expressions correspond in their grammatical form. A parallel such as "He liked to read and to write" (instead of "He liked reading and to write") makes its point neatly. No such neatness appears in "Joyce wrote poems, excellent stories, and novels"; the reader is left wondering what value the poems and novels have. If one of the items has a modifier, usually all should have modifiers. Notice how the omission of "the noble" in the following sentence would leave a distracting gap: "If the wicked Shylock cannot enter the fairy story world of Belmont, neither can the noble Antony." Other examples of parallels: "Mendoza longs to be an Englishman and to marry the girl he loves" (*not* "Mendoza longs to be an Englishman and for the girl he loves"); "He talked about metaphors, similes, and symbols" (*not* "He talked about metaphors, similes, and about symbols"). If one wishes to emphasize the leisureliness of the talk, one might put it thus: "He talked about metaphors, about similes, and about symbols." (The repetition of "about" in this version is not wordiness; because it emphasizes the leisureliness, it does some work in the sentence.) Notice, in the next example, how Miss Gardner's parallels ("in the," "in his," "in his," "in the") lend conviction: "The significance of *Othello* is not to be found in the hero's nobility alone, in his capacity to know ecstasy, in his vision of the world, and in the terrible act to which he is driven by his anguish at the loss of that vision. It lies also in the fact that the vision was true."

Subordination. Make sure that the level of subordination is appropriate to the logical importance of the detail. Make the less important thing subordinate to the more important. Notice how in the following example the first clause, which summarizes the writer's previous sentences, is a dependent clause; the new material is made emphatic by being put into two independent clauses. "As soon as the Irish Literary Theatre was assured of a nationalist backing, it started to dissociate itself from any political aim, and the long struggle with the public began." The second and third clauses in this sentence, linked by "and," are coordinate, that is, of equal importance. We have already discussed parallels ("I came, I saw, I conquered") and pointed out that parallel or coordinate things should appear so grammatically in the sentence. The following line gives time and eternity equal treatment: "Time was against him, eternity was for him." The quotation is a **compound sentence** — two or more clauses that can stand as independent sentences but that are connected with a coordinating conjunction such as *and, but, for, nor, yet,* and *if;* or with a correlative conjunction such as *not only . . . but also;* or with a conjunctive adverb such as *also, however;* or with a colon, semicolon, or (rarely) a comma. But a **complex sentence** (an independent clause and one or more subordinate clauses) does not give equal treatment to each clause; whatever is outside of the independent idea is subordinate. Sample: "Aided by Miss Horniman's money, Yeats dreamed of a poetic drama concentrating on romantic and historical plays." The author puts Yeats's dream in the independent clause and quite rightly subordinates the relatively unimportant Miss Horniman. Had the author wished to give Miss Horniman more prominence, the passage might have run: "Yeats dreamed of a poetic drama concentrating on romantic and historical plays, and this dream was subsidized by Miss Horniman." Here, at least, Miss Horniman stands in an independent clause, linked to the previous independent clause by *and*. (Note, however, that even in the revision Miss Horniman is not very prominent because the subject of the second independent clause is still Yeats's dream — "this dream.") If one wanted to make her yet more prominent one would write, "While Yeats dreamed of a poetic drama concentrating on romantic and historical plays, Miss Horniman provided the means by which the dream might be realized." In short, though simple sentences and compound sentences have their place, they make everything of equal importance. Since everything is not of equal importance, you must often write complex sentences, subordinating some things to other things.

Write Unified and Coherent Paragraphs

Unity. A unified paragraph is a group of sentences (rarely a single sentence) on a single idea. The idea may have several twists or subdivisions, but if you stand back from the paragraph you ought to be able to see that all of the parts — the sentences — are related to form a whole that can be summarized in one sentence. It is, to put the matter a little differently, one of the major points supporting your thesis. If your essay is some five hundred words long — about two double-spaced typewritten pages — it is not likely that you will break it down into more than four or five parts or paragraphs. Each paragraph has a unifying idea, which may appear as a **topic sentence.** Most commonly, the topic sentence is the first sentence in each paragraph, forecasting what is to come in the rest of the paragraph. Less commonly, it is the last sentence in the paragraph, summarizing the points that the paragraph's earlier sentences have made. Least commonly — but thoroughly acceptably — the topic sentence may appear nowhere in the paragraph, in which case it is a

topic idea — an idea that holds the sentences of the paragraph together although it has not been explicitly stated. Whether explicit or implicit, there must be a point that unites the sentences of the paragraph. If your paragraph has only one or two sentences, the chances are that you have not adequately developed the idea of the paragraph.

A paragraph can make several points, but the points must be related, and the nature of the relationship must be indicated so that there is, in effect, a single unifying point to the paragraph. Here is a paragraph, unusually brief, that may seem to make two points but that, in fact, holds them together with an unstated topic idea. The author is Edmund Wilson.

> James Joyce's *Ulysses* was an attempt to present directly the thoughts and feelings of a group of Dubliners through the whole course of a summer day. *Finnegans Wake* is a complementary attempt to render the dream fantasies and the half-unconscious sensations experienced by a single person in the course of a night's sleep.
>
> *The Wound and The Bow* (New York, 1947), p. 243

Wilson's topic idea: *Finnegans Wake* complements *Ulysses*. Notice, by the way, that the sentence about *Finnegans Wake* concludes the paragraph. Not surprisingly, Wilson's essay is about this book, and the structure of the paragraph allows him to get into his subject.

Here is another paragraph that may seem to have more than one subject (Richardson and Fielding were contemporaries; they were alike in some ways; they were different in others), but again the paragraph is unified by a topic idea (although Richardson and Fielding were contemporaries and were alike in some ways, they differed in important ways).

> The names of Richardson and Fielding are always coupled in any discussion of the novel, and with good reason. They were contemporaries, writing in the same cultural climate (*Tom Jones* was published in 1749, a year after *Clarissa*). Both had genius and both were widely recognized immediately. Yet they are utterly different in their tastes and temperaments, and therefore in their visions of city and country, of men and women, and even of good and evil.
>
> Elizabeth Drew, *The Novel* (New York, 1963), p. 59

Notice that this paragraph, like Edmund Wilson's, closes in on its subject.

The beginning and especially the end of a paragraph are usually the most emphatic parts. A beginning may, for example, offer a generalization which the rest of the paragraph supports. Or the early part may offer details, preparing for the generalization in the later part of the paragraph. Or the paragraph may move from cause to effect. Although no rule can cover all paragraphs (except that all must make a point in an orderly way), one can hardly go wrong in making the first sentence of every paragraph either a transition from the previous paragraph or a statement of the paragraph's topic. (But, again, this formula is not inviolable.) Here is a sentence that makes a transition and also states the topic: "Not only narrative poems but also meditative poems may have a kind of plot." This sentence gets the reader from plot in narrative poetry (which the writer has been talking about) to plot in meditative poetry (which the writer goes on to talk about).

Coherence. To say that a paragraph has not only unity but also a structure is to say that the paragraph has coherence. Its parts fit together. Make sure that each sentence is properly related to the preceding one. There is nothing wrong with such obvious **transitions** as "moreover," "however," "but," "for example," "this tendency," "in the next chapter," etc.; but of course 1) these transitions should not start every sentence (they can be buried thus: "Lowell, moreover, . . ."), and 2) they need not appear anywhere in the sentence. The point is not that transitions must be explicit, but that the argument must proceed clearly. The gist of a paragraph might, for example, run thus: "Speaking broadly, there were in the Renaissance two comic traditions . . . . The first . . . . The second . . . . The chief difference . . . . But both traditions . . . ." Here is a paragraph by Elizabeth Drew discussing one aspect of *Great Expectations*. The structure is basically chronological but notice too the effective use of a parallel as a linking device within the last sentence. (The links are italicized.)

> Some of the most poignant scenes in the book are the *opening ones*, which describe the atmosphere in which Pip grows up. *He is introduced* as "a small bundle of shivers" alone in the graveyard, *which is followed* by the terrifying intrusion of the world of active violence and fear as the convict seizes him. *Then we see* the household at the forge, where he is made to feel guilty and ashamed of his very existence; the Christmas party at which he is baited and bullied by his elders; his treatment at the hands of the hypocritical

Pumblechook; his introduction to Estella, who reveals to him that he is coarse and common. *Dickens knows* that in children "there is nothing so finely perceived and so finely felt, as injustice," and looking back on his childhood, *Pip too knows* that truth: "Within myself, I had sustained, from my babyhood, a perpetual conflict with injustice." *The Novel*, p. 197

Introductory and concluding paragraphs. It is especially difficult to lay down rules for writing introductory and concluding paragraphs. The best way to see how they should be handled is to pay attention to them when you read essays, but a few tips may be useful.

When writing an introductory paragraph, try to say something interesting. Don't paraphrase your title in your first sentence: "This theme will study the function of the clown in *Othello*." Don't, on the other hand, be so anxious to say something interesting that you say something irrelevant ("The clowning in *Hamlet* is complex"), or something melodramatic or grandiose ("All the world loves a clown"). Often you can make use of a quotation, either from the work or from a critic; but because the device is a bit too easy, it should be employed only occasionally and with discrimination. You cannot go wrong in suggesting your thesis in your opening paragraph, moving from a rather broad view to a narrower one. Notice, for example, that the introductory paragraph of the essay on *Othello* (p. 10) begins with a sweeping view of the entire dramatis personae of *Othello*, narrows to a view of the clown, and ends with the clear suggestion that the essay will study the work that the clown does in the play. An introductory paragraph can be conceived as a funnel, wide at the top and narrowing into what will be the body of the essay. Here is Nevill Coghill beginning an essay called "Wags, Clowns and Jesters":

Among the less exalted orders of the Shakespearian populace there are three that tend to shade off into a kind of class, whose main functions, mannerisms and idiosyncrasies are easy to recognize, though they tend to merge and mingle, or at least to overlap: they are the Wags, the Clowns and the Jesters.
More Talking of Shakespeare, ed. John Garrett (London, 1959), p. 1

One other kind of introduction should be mentioned, but it is tricky and should be used cautiously. Sometimes an introductory paragraph delicately misleads the audience; the second paragraph reverses the train of thought and leads into the main issue. Here is an example of Joseph Wood Krutch, from *"Modernism" in Modern Drama*. Only the first part of the second paragraph is given below, but you can see what direction Krutch will be taking.

> One evening in 1892, the first of Oscar Wilde's four successful comedies had in London its first performance. It is said that after the last curtain the audience rose to cheer — and it had good reason to do so. Not in several generations had a new play so sparkled with fresh and copious wit of a curiously original kind.
>
> By now the play itself, *Lady Windermere's Fan*, seems thin and faded. To be successfully revived, as it was a few seasons ago in the United States, it has to be presented as "a period piece" — which means that the audience is invited to laugh at as well as with it.
>
> (Ithaca, N.Y., 1953), p. 43

With conclusions, as with introductory paragraphs, try to say something interesting. It is not of the slightest interest to say "Thus we see . . . [here the writer echoes his title and his first paragraph]." There is some justification for a summary at the end of a long paper, where the reader may have half forgotten some of the ideas presented thirty pages earlier, but a paper that can easily be held in the mind needs something different. A good concluding paragraph does more than provide an echo of what the writer has already said. It rounds out the previous discussion, normally with a few sentences that summarize (without the obviousness of "We may now summarize"), but it also may draw an inference that has not previously been expressed. To draw such an inference is not to introduce a new point — a concluding paragraph is hardly the place for a new point — but is to see the previous material in a fresh perspective. A good concluding paragraph closes the issue while enriching it. Notice how the three examples given below all wrap things up and, at the same time, open out by suggesting a larger frame of reference.

The first example is the concluding paragraph of Nevill Coghill's "Wags, Clowns and Jesters":

> "A shrewd knave and an unhappy" is Lafeu's wise comment on Lavache. He is an extreme example of what one finds in so many of Shakespeare's creations — there is more to them than they actually need for the plays in which they appear — they spill over into life.

The second example is the conclusion to Norman Friedman's "Point of View in Fiction," *PMLA*, LXX (1955), 1160–84. In this fairly long discussion of the development of a critical concept, Friedman catalogs various points of view and then spends several pages arguing that the choice of a point of view is crucial if certain effects are to be attained. The omniscient narrator of a novel who comments on all that happens, Friedman suggests, is a sort of free verse of fiction, and an author may willingly sacrifice this freedom for a narrower point of view if he wishes to make certain effects. Friedman concludes:

> All this is merely to say, in effect, that when an author surrenders in fiction, he does so in order to conquer; he gives up certain privileges and imposes certain limits in order the more effectively to render his story-illusion, which constitutes artistic truth in fiction. And it is in the service of this truth that he spends his creative life.

Notice that Friedman devotes the early part of his paragraph to a summary of what has preceded, and then in the latter part he puts his argument in a new perspective. One more example of a concluding paragraph may help to make clear this technique of restating the old and looking toward the new. The paragraph comes from Richard B. Sewall's discussion of *The Scarlet Letter*.

> Henry James said that Hawthorne had "a cat-like faculty of seeing in the dark"; but he never saw through the dark to radiant light. What light his vision reveals is like the fitful sunshine of Hester's and Dimmesdale's meeting in the forest — the tragic opposite of Emerson's triumphant gleaming sun that "shines also today."
>
> *The Vision of Tragedy* (New Haven, 1959), p. 91

Write Emphatically

All that has been said about getting the right word, about effective sentences, and about paragraphs is related to the matter of **emphasis**. But we can add a few points here. The first rule (it will be modified in a moment) is: Be emphatic. But do not attempt to achieve emphasis, as Queen Victoria did, by a *style* consisting *chiefly* of *italics* and *exclamation* marks!!! The proper way to be emphatic is to find the right word, to use appropriate detail, to subordinate the lesser points, and to develop your ideas reasonably. The beginning and the end of a sentence (and of a paragraph) are emphatic positions; of these two positions, the end is usually the more emphatic. Here is a sentence that properly moves to an emphatic end: "Having been ill-treated by Hamlet and having lost her father, Ophelia goes mad." If the halves are reversed, the sentence peters out: "Ophelia goes mad because she has been ill-treated by Hamlet and she has lost her father." Still, even this version is better than the shapeless "Having been ill-treated by Hamlet, Ophelia goes mad, partly too because she has lost her father." The important point, that she goes mad, is dissipated by the lame addition of words about her father. In short, avoid anticlimaxes such as "Macbeth's deed is reprehensible and serious."

But the usual advice, build to emphatic ends, needs modification. Do not write something that sounds like an advertisement for a motion picture: "Into her life came a *man!* He was a *writer!* His name was VOLTAIRE!!" Be emphatic but courteous; do not shout.

One further caution: It is all very well to speak in a courteously low voice, but do not be so timid that you whisper assertions in a negative form. Think twice before you let something like this remain in your manuscript: "Melville is not unsuccessful in his depiction of the pathos of madness." The writer seems reluctant to come out and say "Melville succeeds in depicting the pathos of madness." If this statement needs qualification (e.g., Melville succeeds only in such-and-such a chapter or only intermittently), give the qualifications, but do not think that the weaseling "not unsuccessful" is adequate. It is not unlikely that the reader will not be pleased, which means that it is likely he will be displeased.

SOME REMARKS ABOUT
MANUSCRIPT FORM

Basic Manuscript Form

Much of what follows is nothing more than common sense.

1. Use unlined 8½ × 11 paper of good weight. Keep a carbon copy — onionskin if you wish — but hand in a sturdy original.

2. Double-space, typing (with a reasonably fresh ribbon) on one side of the page only. (If you submit a handwritten copy, use lined paper and write on every other line if the lines are closely spaced.)

3. Leave an adequate margin — an inch or an inch and a half — at top, bottom, and sides.

4. Number the pages consecutively, using Arabic numerals in the upper right-hand corner.

5. Put your name and class or course number in the upper left-hand corner of the first page. It is a good idea to put your name in the upper left corner of each page so that your essay can easily be reassembled if somehow a page gets separated.

6. Center the title of your essay below the top margin of the first page. Begin the first word of the title with a capital, and capitalize each subsequent word except articles, conjunctions, and prepositions, thus: The Diabolic and Celestial Images in *The Scarlet Letter.*

7. Begin the essay an inch or two below the title.

8. Your extensive revisions should have been made in your drafts, but minor last-minute revisions may be made on the finished copy. Proofreading may catch some typographical errors, and you may notice some infelicities. Additions should be made *above* the line, with a caret below the line at the appropriate place. Indicate deletions by drawing a horizontal line through the word or words you wish to delete. Delete a single letter by drawing a vertical line through it. Use a vertical line, too, to separate words that should not have been run together.

Quotations and Quotation Marks

1. Distinguish between short and long quotations, and treat each appropriately. Short quotations (usually defined as less than three lines of poetry or five lines of prose) are enclosed within quotation marks and run into your text (rather than set off, without quotation marks). Examples:

At the conclusion of Milton's "Lycidas," we are told that the shepherd "rose and twitched his mantle blue," suggesting the shepherd's resumption of his usual activity.

Pope's *Essay on Criticism* begins informally with a contraction, but the couplets nevertheless have an authoritative ring: " 'Tis hard to say, if greater want of skill / Appear in writing or in judging ill."

Notice that in the second example a slash (diagonal line, virgule) is used to indicate the end of a line of verse other than the last line quoted. The slash is, of course, not used if the poetry is set off, centered, and printed as verse, thus:

Pope's *Essay on Criticism* begins informally with a contraction, but the couplets nevertheless have an authoritative ring:

> 'Tis hard to say, if greater want of skill
> Appear in writing or in judging ill;
> But of the two less dangerous is the offense
> To tire our patience than mislead our sense.

Material that is set off (usually three or more lines of verse, five or more lines of prose) is not enclosed within quotation marks. To set it off, triple-space before and after the quotation and single-space the quotation. (Some manuals of style call for double-spacing, some for indenting prose quotations. But whichever procedure you adopt, be consistent.) Be sparing in your use of long quotations. Do not bore the reader with material that can be effectively reduced either by paraphrase or by cutting. If you cut, indicate ellipses as explained below under 3.

2. The quotation must fit grammatically into your sentence.

> *Not*: Near the end of the play Othello remembers that he "have done the state some service."
> *Corrected*: Near the end of the play Othello remembers that he has "done the state some service."

3. The quotation must be exact. Any material that you add must be in square brackets, thus:

> When Pope says that Belinda is "the rival of his [i.e., the sun's] beams," he uses comic hyperbole.

Another example:

> Stephen Dedalus sees the ball as a "greasy leather orb [that] flew like a heavy bird through the grey light."

If you wish to omit material from within a quotation, indicate the omission by three spaced periods. If the grammar requires a period after the omission, add a spaced period to the three you have already used to indicate the omission. Here is an example, based on a quotation from the sentences immediately above this one:

> The manual says that "if you . . . omit material from within a quotation, [you must] indicate the omission . . . . If the grammar requires a period . . . add a spaced period . . . .

Notice that although material preceded "If you," periods are not needed to indicate the omission because "If you" began a sentence in the original. Customarily initial and terminal omissions are indicated only when they are part of the sentence you are quoting. Even such omissions need not be indicated when the quoted material is obviously incomplete — when, for instance, it is a word or phrase. (See the first example in this section, which quotes Pope's phrase "the rival of his beams.") Note, too, that although quotations must be given word for word, the initial capitalization can be adapted, as here where "If" is reduced to "if."

4. Commas and periods go inside of the quotation marks; other marks of punctuation (e.g., semicolons, colons, and dashes) go outside. Question marks and exclamation points go inside if they are part of the quotation, outside if they are your own. Examples:

> Amanda ironically says to her daughter, "How old are you, Laura?" Is it possible to fail to hear Laura's weariness in her reply, "Mother, you know my age"?

5. For a quotation contained within a quotation, use *single* quotation marks, thus:

> Later in the essay Henry James says, "They scarcely seem to me to have the quality that Mr. Besant attributes to the rules of the novelist — the 'precision and exactness' of 'the laws of harmony, perspective, and proportion.' "

6. Use quotation marks around titles of short works, that is, for titles of chapters in books, stories, essays, and poems that might not be published by themselves. Unpublished works, even book-length dissertations, are also enclosed in quotation marks. Use *italics* (indicated by underlining) for books, that is, for novels, periodicals, collections of essays, plays, and long poems such as *The Rime of the Ancient Mariner* and *Paradise Lost*.

Footnotes

Kinds of footnotes. Footnotes are of two sorts: 1) they may give the sources of quotations, facts, and opinions used; or 2) they may give additional comment that would interrupt the flow of the argument in the body of the paper. This second type perhaps requires amplification. A writer may wish, for example, to indicate that he is familiar with an opinion contrary to the one he is offering, but he may not wish to digress upon it during the course of his argument. A footnote allows him to refer to it and to indicate why he is not considering it. Or, to take another example, a footnote may contain full statistical data that support his point but that would seem unnecessarily detailed and even tedious in the body of the paper.

What to footnote. Honesty requires that you acknowledge your indebtedness for material, not only when you quote directly from a work, but when you appropriate an idea that is not common knowledge. Not to acknowledge such borrowing is plagiarism. If in doubt as to whether or not to give credit in a footnote, give credit. But you ought to develop a sense of what is considered common knowledge. The date of first publication of *The Scarlet Letter*, for example, can be considered common knowledge. Few can give it when asked, but it can be found out from innumerable sources, and no one need get the credit for providing you with the date. Similarly, the idea that Hamlet delays is a matter of common knowledge. But if, for example, you are impressed by So-and-so's argument that Claudius has been much maligned, you should give credit to So-and-so.

Reducing the number of footnotes. Keep the number of footnotes down to an honest minimum, partly by including the documentation within the body of the paper where reasonable and partly by not cluttering up the bottoms of the pages with references to material that is common knowledge. If, for example, you make frequent quotations from Shakespeare, in the footnote to the first quotation specify which edition you are using and then mention that all subsequent quotations from Shakespeare are from this edition. After each subsequent quotation, put a parenthesis including act, scene, and line (III.ii.178); if you are quoting from various plays, be sure to include the title of the play in the parenthesis. If the quotation is run into the text, close the quotation, give the parenthetic material, and then add the final period. Example:

> The idea that a tragic hero has exhausted all of his life's possibilities is revealed in *Macbeth*, when Malcolm says, "Macbeth/ Is ripe for shaking" (IV.iii.237–38).

If the quotation is set off, end the quotation with a period, double space, and below the last words of the quotation add the parenthetic material. This parenthetic identification, in the body of the paper, does everything that a footnote would do.

The second kind of footnote, which gives additional commentary, should be used sparingly. There are times when supporting details may appropriately be relegated to a footnote, but if the thing is worth saying, it is usually worth saying in the body of the paper. Do not get into the habit of affixing either trivia or miniature essays to the bottom of each page of your essay.

Footnote numbers. Number the notes consecutively through-out the essay or chapter.

Footnote position. Although some instructors allow students to group all of the notes at the rear of the essay, most instructors believe that the best place for a footnote is at the bottom of the appropriate page. If in your draft you type your footnotes on one page, when typing your final copy you can easily gauge how much space the footnotes for any given page will require. Micrometric carbon paper (carbon paper with a protruding margin which bears the line numbers from 64, at the top, down to 1, at the bottom) is a great help.

Footnote style. To indicate that there is a footnote, put a raised Arabic numeral after the final punctuation of the sentence, unless clarity requires it earlier. (In a sentence about Black, Smith, and Jones you may need a footnote for each and a corresponding numeral after each name instead of one at the end of the sentence, but usually a single reference at the end will do. The single footnote might explain that Black says such and such in his book entitled ————, Smith says such and such in his book entitled ————, and Jones says such and such in his book entitled ————.) At the bottom of the page triple-space before giving the first footnote. Then indent five spaces, raise the typewriter carriage half a line, and type the Arabic numeral. Return the carriage to the regular position and type the footnote, single-spacing it. If it runs more than one line, the subsequent lines are flush with the left margin, but each new note begins with an indentation of five spaces. Each note begins with an indented and raised numeral, then a capital letter, and ends with terminal punctuation. Skip a line between footnotes.

First reference to a book. Examples:

[1]X. J. Kennedy, <u>An Introduction to Poetry</u> (Boston, 1966), p. 41.

[2]D. H. Lawrence, <u>Studies in Classic American Literature</u> (New York, 1966), pp. 87-91.

[3]<u>The Letters of John Keats, 1814-1821</u>, ed. Hyder Edward Rollins (Cambridge, Mass., 1958), II, 129.

Notice two points here:

1. Although normally only the city is given, if the city is obscure or might be confused with another city of the same name — as Cambridge, Massachusetts with Cambridge, England — add the necessary amplification, abbreviating if possible.

2. When both volume and page are given, the volume is given in Roman numerals, the page in Arabic numerals. "Vol." and "p." are not used.

[4]Alexander Pope, <u>Epistles to Several Persons</u>, ed. F. W. Bateson, 2nd ed. (New Haven, 1961), p. 17.

[5]Paul Ginestier, <u>The Poet and the Machine</u>, trans. Martin B. Friedman (Chapel Hill, 1961), p. 28.

[6]Albert Gilman and Roger Brown, "Personality and Style in Concord," <u>Transcendentalism and Its Legacy</u>, ed. Myron Simon and Thornton H. Parsons (Ann Arbor, 1966), pp. 103-4.

Notice that the name of an editor or translator is given after the title, with an appropriate abbreviation, as in footnotes 3, 4, 5, 6.

Additional matters:

1. Give the author's name as it appears on the title page; give the title as it appears on the title page, but a very long title may be shortened thus: A *New and Complete Concordance . . . to . . . Shakespeare*; you need not give a subtitle; underline the title of the book, to indicate italics, whatever the typography of the original; if an article, conjunction, or preposition begins the title, capitalize it, but do not capitalize these parts of speech in other places in the title.

2. Although the name of the publisher is not usually given, some instructors require it, thus:

[7]John Malcolm Brinnin, <u>Dylan Thomas in America</u> (Boston: Little, Brown and Co., 1955), p. 98.

3. If the author's name has been given in the body of the page (e.g., in such a sentence as "D. H. Lawrence says that Hawthorne . . ."), do not repeat his name in the footnote. Merely begin with the title. If the author's name and the title have both been given in the body ("D. H. Lawrence says, in *Studies in Classic American Literature*, that Hawthorne . . ."), repeat neither his name nor the title in the footnote. In this case, the footnote would begin with the opening of the parenthesis before the place of publication, thus:

[8](New York, 1966), p. 17.

First reference to a journal. The first example is for a journal paginated consecutively throughout the year, the second is for a journal which paginates each issue individually. A journal paginated separately requires the month or week or day as well as the year. Current practice favors omitting the volume number for popular weeklies (see [11]) and for newspapers, in which case the full date is given without parentheses.

[9] John Oliver Perry, "The Relationship of Disparate Voices in Poems," Essays in Criticism, XV (1965), 49.

[10] T. S. Eliot, "Poetry and Drama," Atlantic, CLXXXVII (February 1951), 30-37.

[11] Bernard McCabe, "Taking Dickens Seriously," Commonweal, May 14, 1965, pp. 244-47.

The author's name and the title of the article are given as they appear in the journal, the title of the article in quotation marks and the title of the journal in italics (i.e., underlined). The volume is given with capital Roman numerals, the page or pages with Arabic numerals.

If a book review has a title, the review may be treated as an article. If, however, the title is merely that of the book reviewed, the following form is commonly used:

[12] Geoffrey Tillotson, rev. of Walter E. Houghton, The Victorian Frame of Mind, 1830-1870 (New Haven, 1957), Victorian Studies, I (1957), 184-85.

Subsequent references. If you quote a second time (or third or fourth) from a work, use a short form. The most versatile short form is simply the author's last name and the page number, thus:

[13] Perry, p. 51.

You can even dispense with the author's name if you have mentioned him in the sentence to which the footnote is keyed. That is, if you have said, "Perry goes on to say . . . ," the footnote need only be

[14] p. 52.

If, however, you have made reference to two different works by the author, you must indicate by a short title which work you are referring to, thus:

[15] Lawrence, Studies, p. 34.

Or, if your sentence mentions that you are quoting Lawrence,

[16] Studies, p. 34.

If you had said something like "Lawrence, in *Studies in Classical American Literature*, argues . . . ," the reference may be merely

[17] p. 34.

In short, a subsequent reference should be as brief as clarity allows. The form *Ibid.* (for *ibidem*, in the same place), indicating that the material being footnoted comes from the same place as the material of the previous footnote, is no longer commonly used. *Op. cit.* (for *opere citato*, in the work cited) and *Loc. cit.* (for *loco citato*, in the place cited), equally unnecessary, have almost disappeared. Identification by author, or by author and short title if necessary, is preferable. A reminder: as p. 44 suggests, if you are going to quote frequently from one source, it will be best to say in your first reference to this source that subsequent quotations from this work will be indicated by parentheses within the body of the paper.

Secondhand references. If you are quoting, say, A. S. F. Gow, but have derived the quotation not from Gow's book but from a book or article that quotes from it, your footnote should indicate both the place where the original quotation may be found and the place where you found it. Example:

[18] A. S. F. Gow, <u>A. E. Housman: A Sketch</u> (New York, 1936), p. 43, quoted in Gilbert Highet, <u>The Classical Tradition</u> (New York, 1949), p. 497.

In this example, Highet's *Classical Tradition* is the book that has been read. If Highet had not given the date or page of Gow's book, and if you have not followed up Highet's lead and looked at Gow's book, your footnote would give only as much information as could be gathered from Highet.

Bibliography

A bibliography is a list of the works cited in the piece of writing or, less often, a list of all of the relevant writing. (There is rarely much point in the second sort; if you have made no use of a particular book or article, why list it?) Normally a bibliography is given only in a long manuscript such as a research paper or a book, but instructors may require a bibliography even for a short paper if they wish to see at a glance the material that the student has used. In this case, a heading such as "Works Consulted" or "Works Cited" is less pretentious than "Bibliography."

Because a bibliography is arranged alphabetically, the author's last name is given first. If a work is by more than one author, the item is given under the first author's name; his last name is given first, but the other author's (or authors') names follow the normal order of first name first. (See the entry under "Wimsatt" below.) Anonymous works are sometimes grouped at the beginning, arranged alphabetically under the first word of the title (or the second word, if the first word is an article), but the recent tendency has been to list them at the appropriate alphabetical place, giving the initial article, if any, but alphabetizing under the next word. Thus, an anonymous article entitled "A View of Faulkner" would retain the "A" but would be alphabetized under V.

In addition to giving the last name first, a bibliography differs from a footnote in putting a period after the author's name; in putting a period after the title of a book and after the number of volumes if more than one; and in not enclosing in parentheses the place and date of publication of a book. And, of course, a bibliographic entry does not include page references for books, though, like a footnote, it includes the page numbers that an essay in a book or in a journal spans. Begin flush with the left-hand margin; if the entry runs over the line, indent the subsequent lines of the entry a few spaces. Double-space between entries. Below are a few samples.

Bush, Douglas. "Wordsworth: A Minority Report," Wordsworth: Centenary Studies, ed. Gilbert T. Dunklin. Princeton, 1951, pp. 3-22.

Fixler, Michael. "The Affinities between J. -K. Huysmans and the 'Rosicrucian' Stories of W. B. Yeats," PMLA, LXXIV (1959), 464-69.

Frye, Northrop. Fables of Identity: Studies in Poetic Mythology. New York, 1963.

____. Fools of Time: Studies in Shakespearian Tragedy. Toronto, 1967.

The horizontal line indicates that the author is the same as in the previous item; multiple titles by one author are arranged alphabetically, as here where *Fables* precedes *Fools*.

Gogol, Nikolai. Dead Souls, trans. Andrew MacAndrew. New York, 1961.

Lang, Andrew. "Ballads," Encyclopaedia Britannica, 11th ed., III, 264-67.

MacCaffrey, Isabel Gamble. Intro. to John Milton, Samson Agonistes and the Shorter Poems. New York, 1966.

This entry suggests that the student made use of the introduction, rather than the main body, of the book; if the body of the book were used, the book would be alphabetized under M for Milton, and the form would resemble that of the next item, with "ed. Isabel Gamble MacCaffrey" following the title.

Pope, Alexander. The Correspondence of Alexander Pope, ed. George Sherburn. 5 vols. Oxford, 1956.

Vendler, Helen. Rev. of Essays on Style, ed. Roger Fowler. Essays in Criticism, XVI (1966), 475-63.

Victorian Poetry and Poetics, ed. Walter E. Houghton and G. Robert Stange. Boston, 1959.

Wimsatt, W. K. Jr., and Cleanth Brooks. Literary Criticism: A Short History. New York, 1957.

A FINAL WARNING:

If you do not master these easy principles, watch out. Montaigne suggests that if a student is stupid or lazy "his tutor should strangle him, if there are no witnesses, or else he should be apprenticed to a pastry-cook in some good town."

PART TWO

3

FICTION

It is usual to say that a narrative — a story, whether a short story or a novel — has an **introduction**, a **complication**, and a **resolution**; that is, it gets under way, some difficulty or problem or complexity arises (usually a **conflict** of opposed wills or forces), and there is some sort of untying or settling-up — or, better, settling-down.[1] These terms can be illustrated most simply in a familiar chestnut, O. Henry's "The Gift of the Magi." We are introduced to a young wife who has only (in addition to a husband) $1.87 and long hair; her husband has only (in addition to a wife) a treasured gold watch. It is the day before Christmas, and gifts must be bought. What to do? As everyone knows, she sells her hair to a wig-maker to buy a watch-fob, only to find that her husband has bought her a set of combs by selling his watch. So

[1] A short story, of course, is not a novel synopsized. A **short story** usually reveals only a single character at a moment of crisis, whereas a **novel** usually traces the development of an individual or a group through cumulative experiences. If the short story is very short, an essayist has a fairly good chance of elucidating the whole, or writing about all of the aspects that seem important to him. But an essayist who writes about a longer story or a novel will have to be content with treating either a few pages or one thread that runs through the work. The last paragraph of this chapter sketches two critical approaches to long fiction.

53

(here is the resolution), these "two foolish children in a flat who most unwisely sacrificed for each other the greatest treasures of their house," smile and set about making dinner. Lest we mistake the author's tone — though his **verbal irony** is unmistakable, for his words clearly mean approximately the opposite of what they say — he adds that "these two were the wisest."

It is usual to say that "The Gift of the Magi" has a clever **plot**. And it does, if by a plot one means something like "a curious happening." It sets forth a cute idea, and no one who reads it ever forgets the idea — the surprising ending. But in one usage of the word plot, "The Gift of the Magi" has scarcely a plot at all. In E. M. Forster's terms, it is only a story (something alleged to have happened), not a plot (happenings that are causally connected). Forster illustrates his distinction thus:

> A plot is also a narrative of events, the emphasis falling on causality. "The king died and then the queen died," is a story. "The king died, and then the queen died of grief" is a plot. The time-sequence is preserved, but the sense of causality overshadows it.
>
> *Aspects of the Novel* (New York), p. 86

In O. Henry's tale, the impact comes from the coincidence of two trains of events (she sells her hair to buy a fob, he sells his watch to buy combs) rather than from the working out of the implications of a deed.

The sense of causality, valued so highly by Forster, is in part rooted in **character**. Things happen, in most good fiction, at least partly because the people have certain personalities or characters and, given their nature, because they respond plausibly to other personalities. As we get to know more about their drives and goals, we enjoy seeing the writer complete the portraits, finally presenting us with a coherent and credible picture of men in action. In this view, plot and character are inseparable. Plot is not simply a series of happenings, but happenings that come out of character, that reveal character, and that influence character. Henry James puts it thus: "What is character but the determination of incident? What is incident but the illustration of character?" But, of course, it is not only what a character does that helps to define him. The narrator often describes him, and the character's words and dress reveal aspects of him. David Lodge's analysis (pp. 131–35) of a page from Dickens' *Hard Times* astutely points out the devices Dickens uses to make us understand what Gradgrind is like.

The writer of fiction provides a coherent world in which the details work together. The **foreshadowing** which would eliminate surprise, or at least greatly reduce it, and thus destroy a story that has nothing else to offer, is a powerful tool in the hands of the writer of serious fiction. Even in such a story as Faulkner's "A Rose for Emily," where we are surprised to learn near the end that Miss Emily has slept beside the decaying corpse of her dead lover, from the outset we expected something strange; that is, we are not surprised by the surprise, only by its precise nature. The first sentence of the story tells us that after Miss Emily's funeral (the narrator begins at the end) the townspeople crossed the threshold "out of curiosity to see the inside of her house, which no one save an old manservant . . . had seen in at least ten years." As the story progresses, we see Miss Emily prohibiting people from entering the house, we hear that after a certain point no one ever saw Homer Barron again, that "the front door remained closed," and (a few paragraphs before the end of the story) that the townspeople "knew that there was one room in that region above the stairs which no one had seen in forty years." The paragraph preceding the revelation that "the man himself lay in bed" is devoted to a description of Homer's dust-covered clothing and toilet articles. In short, however much we are unprepared for the precise revelation, we are prepared for some strange thing in the house; and, given Miss Emily's purchase of poison and Homer's disappearance, we have some idea of what might be revealed.

Let us take another example of a story in which the beginning is a preparation for all that follows. Consider, for example, the first two paragraphs of Joyce's "Araby."

> North Richmond Street, being blind, was a quiet street except at the hour when the Christian Brothers' school set the boys free. An uninhabited house of two storeys stood at the blind end, detached from its neighbours in a square ground. The other houses of the street, conscious of decent lives within them, gazed at one another with brown imperturbable faces.
>
> The former tenant of our house, a priest, had died in the back drawing-room. Air, musty from having been long enclosed, hung in all the rooms, and the waste room behind the kitchen was littered with old useless papers. Among these I found a few paper-covered books, the pages of which were curled and damp: *The Abbot*, by Walter Scott, *The Devout Communicant* and *The Memoirs of Vidocq*. I liked the last best because its leaves were yellow. The wild

garden behind the house contained a central apple-tree and a few
straggling bushes under one of which I found the late tenant's rusty
bicycle-pump. He had been a very charitable priest; in his will he
had left all his money to institutions and the furniture of his house
to his sister.

A dead-end ("blind") street contains "imperturbable" houses,
including an uninhabited one. The former tenant of the house
that the narrator lived in was a priest who died in the back
drawing-room, leaving, among other things, musty air, yellow-
ing books, and a rusty bicycle pump. If we have read with any
care, we find that Joyce indeed gives us in these paragraphs a
vision of the paralysis of Ireland that he elsewhere speaks of.
As we read further in the story, we are not surprised to learn
that the boy for a while manufactured quasi-religious experiences
(religion being dead — remember the priest and his rusty bicycle pump). In his ears, shop-boys sing "litanies," his girl
friend's name springs to his lips "in strange prayers," and his
vision of her is a "chalice" which he carries "safely through a
throng of foes." He plans to visit a bazaar, and he promises to
bring her a gift; but after he has with some difficulty arrived at
the bazaar, he is vastly disappointed by the trivial conversation of
the attendants, by the counting of the day's receipts (money-
changers in the temple), and by the darkness ("the upper part
of the hall was now completely dark"). The last line of the story
runs thus: "Gazing up into the darkness I saw myself as a creature driven and derided by vanity; and my eyes burned with
anguish and anger." Everything in the story coheres; the dead-
end street, the dead priest, the rusty pump — all are perfect
preludes to this story about a boy's recognition of the nothingness that surrounds him. (The "vanity" that drives and derides
him is not only the egotism that moved him to think he could
bring the girl a fitting gift but also the nothingness that is spoken
of in the biblical "Vanity of vanities, all is vanity.")

An essay on foreshadowing will almost surely work through
the evidence chronologically, though of course the initial paragraph may discuss the end and indicate that the remainder of
the essay will be concerned with tracing the way in which the
author prepares the reader for this end and the way in which he
simultaneously maintains the right amount of suspense. If the
suspense is too slight, we stop reading, not caring what comes
next. If too great, we are perhaps reading a story in which the

interest depends entirely on some strange happening rather than a story with sufficiently universal application to make it worthy of a second reading. The essay will study the way in which details gain in meaning as the reader gets further into the story. Or it may study the author's failure to keep his details relevant and coherent, his tendency to introduce material for its momentary value at the expense of the larger design. An essay on an uneven story may do both: it may show that although there are unfortunate irrelevancies, there is also considerable skill in arousing and interestingly fulfilling the reader's expectations. If the essayist feels that the story is fundamentally successful, the organization of his thoughts might reflect his feelings. After an initial paragraph in which he states his overall position, he will probably discuss the failures and then go on, at greater length, to discuss the strengths, thus ending strongly on his main point. If he feels that the story is essentially a failure, he will probably first briefly discuss its merits and then go on to his main point, the unsatisfactory nature of the story. To reverse this procedure, clearly, would be to leave the reader with an impression contrary to the essayist's thesis.

Foreshadowing normally makes use of **setting.** The setting or environment in the first two paragraphs of Joyce's "Araby" is not mere geography, not mere locale: it provides an **atmosphere,** an air that the characters breathe, a world in which they move. Some familiar examples from Thomas Hardy's novels may clarify the point. In *Tess of the D'Urbervilles* we are told of a place called Flintcomb Ash, where "the whole field was in color a desolate drab; it was a complexion without features, as if a face, from chin to brow, should be only an expanse of skin. The sky wore, in another color, the same likeness; a white vacuity of expression with the lineaments gone." Or, again, near the end of the novel, when, just before her arrest, Tess lies upon a great stone slab at Stonehenge, she is associated with all of the victims of history and prehistory. Dorothy Van Ghent calls attention to the role that the earth plays in *Tess.* There are

> the long stretches of earth that have to be trudged in order that a person may get from one place to another, the slowness of the business, the irreducible reality of it (for one has only one's feet), its grimness of soul-wearying fatigue and shelterlessness and doubtful issue at the other end of the journey where nobody may be at home.
> *The English Novel* (New York, 1953), p. 201

Mrs. Van Ghent goes on to say, in discussing *The Mayor of Casterbridge*:

> The Roman ruins round about the town of Casterbridge are a rather
> . . . complicated metaphor, for they are works of man that have
> fallen into earth; they speak mutely of the anonymity of human
> effort in historical as well as in geological times; their presence sug-
> gests also the classic pattern of the Mayor's tragedy, the ancient
> repetitiveness of self-destruction; and they provide thus a kind of
> guarantee or confirming signature of the heroism of the doomed
> human enterprise.

David Lodge, on pp. 131–33, points out that Dickens' "plain, bare, monotonous vault of a schoolroom," the domain of the schoolmaster Gradgrind, is a kind of extension of Gradgrind himself, who has a "square wall of a forehead," an "inflexible" voice, and a "square coat." In short, in a good piece of fiction the setting is not merely "colorful" but relevant.

In "Composition and Fate in the Short Novel," using Thomas Mann's "Death in Venice" as an illustration, Howard Nemerov distinguishes between two kinds of relevance in literature:

> One kind has to do with the temporal succession of events, as
> though the single point of the idea must be viewed in an added
> dimension as a straight line; in order to tell how a distinguished
> German author dies in Venice we must get him to Venice, keep
> him there, and supply a disease for him to die of. He will doubtless
> see many things, and think many things, on his journey — what
> things? We need another kind of relevance, having to do with as-
> sociation, symbol, metaphor, as well as with probable and realistic
> observation; while the distinguished author is in Venice it occurs
> to him, waking, that his situation is like that discussed in the
> *Phaedrus*, and dreaming, that his situation is like that of King
> Pentheus in *The Bacchae* of Euripides.   *Poetry and Fiction: Essays*
> (New Brunswick, 1963), pp. 241–42

Without this first kind of relevance, of course, there is no story; without the second kind it is a different story. The story we value has both kinds. Nemerov continues with his illustration from "Death in Venice":

> When Aschenbach dies, there by the shore, we are told that the
> weather was autumnal, the beach deserted and not even very clean;
> suddenly we are given this: "A camera on a tripod stood at the edge
> of the water, apparently abandoned; its black cloth snapped in the
> freshening wind." That is all, our attention is given to Tadzio,
> Aschenbach's death soon follows, the camera is never mentioned
> again.

Crudely speaking, this camera is unnecessary and no one could possibly have noticed anything missing had the author decided against its inclusion; yet in a musical, compositional sense it exquisitely touches the center of the story and creates a resonance which makes us for a moment aware of the entire inner space of the action, of all things relevant and their relations to one another.

Our sense of this is mostly beyond exposition, as symbolic things have a way of being; but some of its elements may be mentioned. About the camera by the sea there is, first, a poignant desolation, the emptiness of vast spaces, and in its pictorial quality it resembles one of the earliest images in the story, when Aschenbach, standing by the cemetery, looks away down the empty streets: "not a wagon in sight, either on the paved Ungererstrasse, with its gleaming tramlines stretching off towards Schwabing, nor on the Föhring highway." Both pictures are by Di Chirico. The camera's black cloth reminds us of the gondola, "black as nothing else on earth except a coffin," and the repeated insistence on black in that description; also of the "labor in darkness" which brings forth the work of art. For we perceive that the camera stands to the sea as, throughout this story, the artist has stood to experience, in a morally heroic yet at the same time dubious or ridiculous or even impossible relation of form to all possibility, and that at the summer's end, in the freshening wind, the camera is abandoned. It would be near forgivable, so full of Greek mysteries is this work, if we thought the tripod itself remotely Delphic.

It is not enough, of course, to weave a pattern of references, a chain of images. (An essay that merely catalogs references to blackness in "Death in Venice" will not be of much interest.) The writer's story must be about something; and his language is the net that catches it, the device whereby he makes something we value, something which says something about human experience. This intangible he gives us has been called "felt life" and "felt reality." Here is a paragraph by another critic, Martin Green, sharply criticizing Hawthorne for naming experiences rather than catching them. Green begins by quoting from Hawthorne's "Young Goodman Brown."

"On he flew among the black pines, brandishing his staff with frenzied gestures, now giving vent to an inspiration of horrid blasphemy, and now shouting forth such laughter as set all the echoes of the forest laughing like demons around him." Nothing there evokes the experience of blasphemy. Everything evokes memories of fanciful fiction. "Another verse of the hymn arose, a low and mournful strain, such as the pious love, but joined to words which expressed all that our natures can conceive of sin, and darkly hinted at far more." This is the language of empty exaggeration; after all that our natures can conceive comes "far more." "Young Goodman Brown" is not an allegory because it allegorizes nothing. There is no experience embodied in its language, and consequently no reason to construct elaborate meanings for its oddities.

                                    Re-appraisals (New York, 1965), pp. 73–74

Green may be wrong, but notice how he makes his point: he begins with a quotation from the story, offers his criticism, and then offers another quotation that allows him to restate his criticism. He concludes the paragraph with yet another and broader restatement.

An "experience," of course, is not a happening through which the author necessarily passed; rather, it is a thought, an emotion, a vision that is meaningful and is embodied in the piece of fiction for all to read. Inevitably the writer uses **symbols** (the blackness, the camera, and the beach that Nemerov comments on). Symbols are neither puzzles nor colorful details but are among the concrete embodiments that give the story whatever accuracy it has. Joyce's dead-end street, dead priest, apple tree (suggestive of the Garden of Eden, now fallen?), and rusty bicycle pump all help to define very precisely the condition of a thoroughly believable Dublin. In an analysis of "The Dead," another of Joyce's stories, David Daiches suggests (p. 141),

> The snow, which falls indifferently upon all things, covering them with a neutral whiteness and erasing all their differentiating details, is the symbol of Gabriel's new sense of identity with the world, of the breakdown of the circle of his egotism to allow him to become for the moment not a man different from all other men living in a world of which he alone is the center but a willing part of the general flux of things.

Mary McCarthy, in an essay on symbolism, points out that symbols are not odd things stuck into a story but are things that properly belong in the world of the story. She effectively illustrates her point with an example from Tolstoy's *Anna Karenina*.

> Toward the beginning of the novel, Anna meets the man who will be her lover, Vronsky, on the Moscow-St. Petersburg express; as they meet, there has been an accident; a workman has been killed by the train. This is the beginning of Anna's doom, which is completed when she throws herself under a train and is killed; and the last we see of Vronsky is in a train, with a toothache; he is off to the wars.

The train is necessary to the plot of the novel, and I believe it is also symbolic, both of the iron forces of material progress that Tolstoy hated so and that played a part in Anna's moral destruction, and also of those iron laws of necessity and consequence that govern human action when it remains on the sensual level.

One can read the whole novel, however, without being conscious that the train is a symbol; we do not have to "interpret" to feel the import of doom and loneliness in the train's whistle — the same import we ourselves can feel when we hear a train whistle blow in the country, even today.   *On the Contrary* (New York, 1962), p. 236

The symbols, to repeat, are a part of the world of the story, contributing to its sense of immediacy or reality as well as radiating suggestions or (to use Henry James's figure) casting long shadows. In Hardy's *Jude the Obscure*, for example, the pigeons that Jude and Sue are forced to sell are symbols of Jude's and Sue's caged existence, but they are also pigeons that Jude and Sue are forced to sell. Furthermore, other references to birds in the novel function similarly, as do the passages dealing with the trapped rabbit. Birds and rabbits are a part of Jude's world, meaningful on the realistic level but resonant too. An essayist who discusses symbolism in a piece of fiction will probably want to examine the degree to which the symbols are integral and interrelated.

The Dublin in "Araby" and the England in *Jude* are the Dublin and England that Joyce and Hardy thought existed, but it must be remembered that although an author *writes* a story, someone else *tells* it. The story is seen from a particular **point of view**. A wide variety of terms has been established to name differing points of view, but the following labels are among the commonest. We can begin with two categories: third-person points of view (in which the narrator is, in the crudest sense, not a character in the story) and first-person points of view (in which the "I" who narrates the story plays a part in it).

The **third-person point of view** itself has several subdivisions. At one extreme is the **omniscient narrator**. He knows everything that is going on; he can tell us the inner thoughts of all of the characters. He may editorialize, passing judgments, reassuring his reader, etc., in which case he may sound like the author. Here is Hardy's omniscient narrator in *Tess of the D'Urbervilles*, telling the reader that Tess was mistaken in imagining that the countryside proclaimed her guilt: "But this encompassment of her own characterization, based upon shreds of convention, peopled by phantoms and voices antipathetic to her, was a sorry and mistaken creation of Tess's fancy — a cloud of moral hobgoblins by which she was terrified without reason." Still, even this narrator is not quite Hardy; he does not allude to his other books, his private life, or his hope that the book will sell. If he is Hardy, he is only one aspect of Hardy, quite possibly a fictional Hardy, a disembodied voice with particular characteristics.

Another sort of third-person narrator (**selective omniscient**) takes up what Henry James called a "center of consciousness," revealing the thoughts of one of the characters but (for the most part) seeing the rest of the characters from the outside only. Wayne Booth, in a penetrating study of Jane Austen's *Emma*, explains the effectiveness of selective omniscience in this novel. He points out that Emma is intelligent, witty, beautiful, and rich. But she is flawed by pride, and, until she discovers and corrects her fault, she almost destroys herself and her friends. How to make such a character sympathetic, so that we will hope for the happy conclusion to the comedy? "The solution to the problem of maintaining sympathy despite almost crippling faults," Booth says,

> was primarily to use the heroine herself as a kind of narrator, though in third person, reporting on her own experience . . . . By showing most of the story through Emma's eyes, the author insures that we shall travel with Emma rather than stand against her. It is not simply that Emma provides, in the unimpeachable evidence of her own conscience, proof that she has many redeeming qualities that do not appear on the surface; such evidence could be given with authorial commentary, though perhaps not with such force and conviction. Much more important, the sustained inside view leads the reader to hope for good fortune for the character with whom he travels, quite independently of the qualities revealed.
>
> *The Rhetoric of Fiction* (Chicago, 1961), pp. 245–46

Booth goes on to point out, in a long and subtle analysis, that "sympathy for Emma can be heightened by withholding inside views of others as well as by granting them of her."

In writing about point of view, one of course tries to suggest what the author's choice of a particular point of view contributes to the story. Wayne Booth, we have just seen, shows how Jane Austen's third-person point of view helps to keep sympathetic a character who otherwise might be less than sympathetic. Booth states the problem — how to draw an intelligent but proud woman so that the reader will wish for a happy ending — and he presents his answer convincingly, moving from "It is not simply . . ." to "Much more important." (To reverse the order would cause a drop in interest.) He then moves from a discussion of the inside treatment of Emma to the outside treatment of the other characters, thus substantiating and enlarging his argument. Possibly one could reverse this procedure, beginning with a discussion of the treatment of the characters other than Emma and then closing in on Emma, but such an essay may seem slow in getting under way. The early part may appear unfocused. The reader will for a while be left wondering why in an essay on point of view in *Emma* the essayist does not turn to the chief matter, the presentation of the central character.

To continue our discussion of kinds of points of view: the third-person narrator, then, although not in the ordinary sense a character in the story, is an important voice in the story, who helps to give shape to it. Another type of third-person narrator is the so-called **effaced narrator.** He does not seem to exist, for he does not comment in his own voice (unlike the editorially omniscient narrator), and he does not enter any minds (unlike the omniscient or selective omniscient narrator). The reader hears dialogue and sees only what a camera or a fly on the wall would see. Sample, from Hemingway's "The Killers":

> The door of Henry's lunchroom opened and two men came in. They sat down at the counter.
> "What's yours?" George asked them.
> "I don't know," one of the men said. "What do you want to eat, Al?"
> "I don't know," said Al. "I don't know what I want to eat."

But even an effaced narrator has, if we think a moment, a kind of personality. The story he records may seem "cold" or "scientific" or "reportorial" or "objective," and such a **tone** or voice (attitude of the narrator, as it is detected) may be an important part of the story. Rémy de Gourmont's remark, quoted in Ezra Pound's *Literary Essays*, is relevant: "To be impersonal is to be personal in a special kind of way . . . . The objective is one of the forms of the subjective."

To turn to **first-person,** or **participant, points of view:** the

"I" who narrates a story (recall that at the end of "Araby" the narrator says, "I saw myself as a creature driven and derided by vanity") may be a major character in it (as he is in "Araby," in *The Catcher in the Rye,* and in Dickens' *Great Expectations*), or he may be a minor character, a mere witness (Nick Carroway narrates the story of Gatsby in *The Great Gatsby*). A first-person narrator may not fully understand his own report. This is the **innocent-eye** device, in which a good part of the effect consists in the discrepancy between the narrator's imperfect awareness and the reader's superior awareness. The classic example is the narrator of Ring Lardner's "Haircut," a barber, who, thinking he is describing an accident, actually (the reader understands) describes a murder. Although we sometimes feel that a first-person narrator (Conrad's Marlow in several novels is an example) is a very thinly veiled substitute for the author, the words of a first-person narrator require the same kind of scrutiny that we give to the words of the other characters in a story or play. The reader must deduce the personality from what is said. The narrator of "Araby," for instance, never tells us that he was a good student; but, from such a passage as this, we can deduce that he was a bookish boy until he fell in love: "I watched my master's face pass from amiability to sternness; he hoped I was not beginning to idle." A first-person narrator is not likely to give us the help that an editorially omniscient narrator gives. We must deduce that his uncle drinks too much from this passage: "At nine o'clock I heard my uncle's latchkey in the hall-door. I heard him talking to himself and heard the hall-stand rocking when it had received the weight of his overcoat. I could interpret these signs."

In a first-person narrative it is sometimes difficult for the reader to interpret the signs. In a sense the author has given the reader two stories: the story the narrator tells and a second story, the story of a narrator telling a story. Suppose we have decided to write about point of view in Henry James's ghost story, *The Turn of the Screw.* We notice, first of all, that it is told in the first person, beginning thus:

> The story had held us, round the fire, sufficiently breathless, but except the obvious remark that it was gruesome, as, on Christmas eve in an old house, a strange tale should essentially be, I remember no comment uttered till somebody happened to say that it was the only case he had met in which such a visitation had fallen on a child.

Our unnamed narrator — we can call him Henry James, but only if we remember that he exists here only as narrator, not as the American expatriot, the brother of William James, etc. — is one of a group which has heard a ghost story. He goes on to introduce us to another member of the group, someone named Douglas:

> It was this observation that drew from Douglas — not immediately, but later in the evening — a reply that had the interesting consequence to which I call attention.

The narrator proceeds to tell us that two nights later Douglas told a ghost story concerning a governess and her two charges, a boy and a girl, who had been harried by the ghosts of two former servants. Douglas did not exactly tell the story, rather he read it from a manuscript written long ago by the governess. There are, then, three narrators: the "I" who addresses the reader; Douglas, who narrates the ghost story; and the governess, whose words Douglas reads aloud to the group. The heart of *The Turn of the Screw* is, therefore, the governess' long first-person narrative, which is read to a group by Douglas and which is recounted to the reader by one of the group, "I." If an essayist is writing about point of view in James's story, he will want to comment on this narrator within a narrator within a narrator. He will want to ask himself at least two questions: What broad effects does this framework have on the reader, and how reliable are Douglas and the governess as narrators?

Because the first question is simpler and less important, it is probably best to treat it first and get on to the larger matter. An essay might, then, at the outset, touch on the suitability of having a ghost story told by someone who has heard it from someone who saw the ghosts. Ghost stories are like that; we usually get them not firsthand but second- or thirdhand, and we listen with wonder and at the same time with a sense of doubt. The stories, like ghosts, are not within our grasp; we wish we could question the eyewitness, but we cannot. Having said this much, the essayist might add that because ghost stories belong primarily to the world of oral literature, where stories are told to a group rather than read by an individual, it is appropriate for this story, too, to be told to a group. James's first line, "The story had held us, round the fire," in some measure takes us into the world of oral literature, a world less intellectual than the world of books. Even this outermost narrator is simply one of "us," a nameless part of the community, a member of Douglas' audience two nights later.

The writer of an essay on point of view in *The Turn of the Screw* will next alert his reader to the fact that he has finished his discussion of the broad effects created by the framework and will now turn to the second, and more important, point: the degree to which the narrators' personalities color the events. Douglas explains that he met the governess when he was a university student; she was ten years older than he, and she seemed "worthy" and "clever"; he "liked her extremely." He means to assure his audience of her reliability, but the reader senses that Douglas was infatuated with her; the reader learns, too, that Douglas did not meet her until ten years after her ordeal with the ghosts, when she was no longer an "anxious girl out of a Hampshire vicarage," "young, untried, nervous." The essayist may decide that her personality indeed colors the happenings. If he does, he will collect the details about her provincial background and her inexperience, which made awesome the responsibility of bringing up two children. He will probably devote a paragraph to what he understands her intellectual and emotional state to have been at the time she accepted the job. If he sees her as unprepared and unstable, he will want to explain that Douglas' positive remarks about her must be taken only provisionally and as only Douglas' view; the real governess is not simply the "worthy" girl Douglas thinks he is describing, but she is the governess whom the reader perceives through Douglas' words and through her own. The essayist will give the evidence that supports his own view that she was unstable: various bits that emphasize her naiveté and her nervousness provide the background. Then he will go on to examine her less direct revelations. At one point, for example, she compares herself and the little boy in her charge to "some young couple on their wedding-journey." He might notice that she sometimes says "I felt" and later reports as a fact the thing she had only "felt," and that she is given to learning things in a "flash of knowledge" rather than in a more acceptable way. An essayist on this topic will notice, too, the lack of corroboration. The governess insists that the little girl saw the ghost, and she explains that the girl would lie and deny it if asked; there is, then, in her opinion, no need to check with the girl. The essayist might well conclude that the story is two stories: a ghost story and also the story of a neurotic woman who may — or may not — have seen ghosts.

In this sketch of an essay on point of view in *The Turn of the Screw*, one important matter may have been omitted: Is there any evidence, other than Douglas' testimony of the governess' good character, that conflicts with the thesis that she is neurotic? If there is, it must, of course, be accounted for. *Where* it will be accounted for depends upon what it is. As we have seen, Douglas' testimony can effectively be given immediately after the discussion of Douglas as a narrator and before the essayist's detailed discussion of the governess. About the only advice one can give is to put it at the appropriate place, the place where the reader *ought* to be told. Usually, as with the comment on Douglas' comments, it should precede your detailed refutation; if it follows, your essay may seem to run downhill. But in initially setting forth a position that will be refuted, the reader should be given a clear hint of what is to come; there is no point in setting forth an argument that at first seems convincing only to inform the reader that he has accepted an insubstantial argument. A clue such as "It may seem," or "Although at first glance one may believe," will often be enough, though sometimes one may want to be even more forthright: "The argument that the governess is reliable is based on two pieces of evidence, but neither is substantial. The first . . . ." Usually the most satisfactory formula is to state your view at some length, take account of the objections at the points where they might reasonably be offered, and move steadily toward developing your thesis.

Because modern fiction makes subtle use of point of view, it can scarcely be neglected in a discussion of what a story is about. Perhaps unfairly, modern criticism is usually unhappy with suggestions of the author's voice in older fiction. We would rather see than be lectured at. We are less impressed by "It was the stillness of an implacable force brooding over an inscrutable intention" than by this passage (also from Conrad's *Heart of Darkness*):

> Black shapes crouched, lay, sat between the trees, leaning against the trunks, clinging to the earth, half coming out, half effaced within the dim light, in all the attitudes of pain, abandonment, and despair.

> Another mine on the cliff went off, followed by a slight shudder of the soil under my feet. The work was going on. The work! And this was the place where some of the helpers had withdrawn to die.

The second quotation, but not the first, gives us the sense of reality that we have come to expect from fiction. (Still, this is a critical assumption that can be questioned.) Hardy's novels in particular have been censured on this account; the modern sensibility is uneasy when it hears Hardy's own voice commenting on the cosmic significance of the happenings, as when in *Tess of the D'Urbervilles* the narrator says: "In the ill-judged execution of the well-judged plan of things, the call seldom produces the comer, the man to love rarely coincides with the hour for loving." The passage goes on in this vein at some length. Even in passages of dialogue we sometimes feel that we are getting not a vision of life but a discourse on it, as in this famous exchange between Tess and her brother:

> "Did you say the stars were worlds, Tess?"
> "Yes."
> "All like ours?"
> "I don't know; but I think so. They sometimes seem to be like the apples on our stubbard-tree. Most of them splendid and sound — a few blighted."
> "Which do we live on — a splendid one or a blighted one?"
> "A blighted one."

We prefer the picture of the field at Flintcomb Ash, the pigeons, the rabbits, Stonehenge. Partly, we feel, overt commentary (even when put into the mouths of the characters) leaves the world of fiction and invites us to judge it separately, as philosophy. Partly, of course, the difficulty is that twentieth-century novelists and readers have come to expect the novel to do something different from what Hardy and his contemporaries expected it to do. As Virginia Woolf puts it in "Mr. Bennett and Mrs. Brown," the novelists before the first world war "made tools and established conventions which do their business. But those tools are not our tools, and that business is not our business. For us those conventions are ruin, those tools are death." Mrs. Van Ghent concisely gives the modern objection: when the philosophic vision

> can be loosened away from the novel to compete in the general field of abstract truth — as frequently in Hardy — it has the weakness of any abstraction that statistics and history and science may be

allowed to criticize; whether true or false for one generation or another, or for one reader or another, or even for one personal mood or another, its status as truth is relative to conditions of evidence and belief existing outside the novel and existing there quite irrelevant to whatever body of particularized life the novel itself might contain.

The English Novel, p. 197

Mrs. Van Ghent goes on to explain that the philosophic vision has its proper place in the novel when it is "local and inherent there through a maximum of organic dependencies." She illustrates her point by quoting this passage from *Tess*, which describes the coming of morning after Tess's horse has been accidentally stabbed to death by the shaft of a mail cart.

The atmosphere turned pale, the birds shook themselves in the hedges, arose, and twittered; the lane showed all its white features, and Tess showed hers, still whiter. The huge pool of blood in front of her was already assuming the iridescence of coagulation; and when the sun rose, a million prismatic hues were reflected from it. Prince lay alongside still and stark, his eyes half open, the hole in his chest looking scarcely large enough to have let out all that had animated him.

Part of Mrs. Van Ghent's comment runs thus:

With the arousal and twittering of the birds we are aware of the oblivious manifold of nature stretching infinite and detached beyond the isolated human figure; the iridescence of the coagulating blood is, in its incongruity with the dark human trouble, a note of the same indifferent cosmic chemistry that has brought about the accident; and the smallness of the hole in Prince's chest, that looked "scarcely large enough to have let out all that had animated him," is the minor remark of that irony by which Tess's great cruel trial appears as a vanishing incidental in the blind waste of time and space and biological repetition. Nevertheless, there is nothing in this event that has not the natural "grain" of concrete fact; and what it signifies — of the complicity of doom with the most random occurrence, of the cross-purposing of purpose in a multiple world, of cosmic indifference and of moral desolation — is a local truth of a particular experience and irrefutable as the experience itself.

The English Novel, pp. 198–99

In attempting to take account of the **theme** of a work of fiction (What does it add up to? What is the motif that holds the happenings together? What is the point? *Not*: How does it turn out? *Not:* What happens?),[2] the essayist must consider the role of such concrete facts. Suppose we look briefly at James Joyce's "The Dead." The narrative tells of Gabriel's arrival at a party, the events at the party, his subsequent departure, and his realization that his wife was taken up with the thought of a boy, unknown to Gabriel, who had loved her. As David Daiches points out (p. 136) in his essay on the theme of this story, about three-fourths of the story is devoted to episodes at the party. Daiches suggests that these episodes modify each other and embody the theme. That theme, he says, is the liberation of Gabriel from his own egotism. Here is the skeleton of Daiches' essay:

> The theme of "The Dead" is the liberation of Gabriel from his own egotism; this theme determines the episodes:
>
> > The first attack on his egotism (the caretaker's daughter is not impressed by him)
> >
> > Gabriel's response (he is a little distressed)
> >
> > The second attack (Miss Ivors attacks his individualism and questions his patriotism)
> >
> > Gabriel's response (he is distressed, but he calms himself by denigrating her, and he regains his composure when he sits at the head of the table)
> >
> > The third attack (D'Arcy's favorable reference to Caruso reveals the provincialism of the rest of the group, whose members have hardly heard of him)
> >
> > Gabriel continues in his role as the center of attention
> >
> > The fourth attack (D'Arcy's singing and playing take the limelight from Gabriel)
> >
> > The fifth attack (confident and desirous of his wife, Gabriel learns that her thoughts are of a boy he does not even know)
> >
> > Gabriel's response (humbled, he dozes off and becomes a part of all the blank, snow-covered world around him)

---

[2] A theme in a literary work is not a thesis, an arguable message such as "Men ought not to struggle against fate"; rather, it is something like "Man's Struggle against Fate" or "The Process of Growing Up" or "The Quest for Knowledge." The formulation of a theme normally includes an abstract noun or a phrase. For some further comments on theme, see pp. 80–82.

4

DRAMA

WRITING
ABOUT DRAMA

Most of the world's great plays may be put into one of two classes: tragedy and comedy. Roughly speaking, tragedy dramatizes the conflict between the vitality of the single life and the laws or limits of life (the tragic hero reaches his heights, going beyond the experiences of other men, at the cost of his life), and comedy dramatizes the vitality of the laws of social life (the good life is seen to reside in the shedding of individualism in favor of a union with a genial and enlightened society). These points must be amplified a bit before we go on to the further point that, of course, any important play does much more than can be put into such crude formulas.

In **tragedy,** usually, the tragic hero goes beyond the standards to which reasonable men adhere; he does some fearful deed which ultimately destroys him but at the same time shows him (paradoxically) to be in some way more fully a living being — a man who has experienced life more fully, whether by heroic action or by capacity for enduring suffering — than the men around him. Othello kills Desdemona, Lear gives away his crown and banishes his one loving daughter, Antony loses his share of the Roman Empire; but all of these men seem to live more fully — for one thing, they experience a kind of anguish

75

unknown to those who surround them and who outlive them.
(If the hero does not die, he usually is left in some death-like
state, as is the blind Oedipus in *King Oedipus*.) We see humanity pushed to an extreme; in his agony and grief the hero
enters a world unknown to the rest and reveals magnificence.
After his departure from the stage, we are left in a world of
littler men. The closing lines of almost any of Shakespeare's
tragedies can be used to illustrate the point. *King Lear*, for example, ends thus:

> The oldest hath borne most: we that are young
> Shall never see so much, nor live so long.

Tragedy commonly involves **irony** of two sorts: unconsciously
ironic deeds and unconsciously ironic speeches. **Ironic deeds** have
some consequence more or less the reverse of what the doer in-
tends. Examples: Macbeth thinks that by killing Duncan he will
gain happiness, but he finds that his deed brings him sleepless
nights. Brutus thinks that by killing Caesar he will bring liberty
to Rome, but he brings tyranny. In an unconsciously **ironic
speech**, the speaker's words mean one thing to him but something more significant to the audience, as when King Duncan,
baffled by Cawdor's treason, says:

> There's no art
> To find the mind's construction in the face:
> He was a gentleman on whom I built
> An absolute trust.

At this moment Macbeth, whom we have already heard meditating the murder of Duncan, enters. Duncan's words are true,
but he does not apply them to Macbeth, as the audience does.
A second example of an unconsciously ironic speech: A few
moments later Duncan praises Macbeth as "a peerless kinsman."
Soon Macbeth will indeed become peerless, when he kills Duncan and ascends to the throne.[1] Sophocles' use of ironic deeds

---

[1] Ironic deeds, or happenings, and unconsciously ironic speeches must
be distinguished from **verbal irony,** which is produced when the speaker
is conscious that his words mean something different from what they
say. Example: In *Macbeth* Lennox says: "The gracious Duncan /
Was pitied of Macbeth. Marry, he was dead! / And the right valiant
Banquo walked too late. / . . . / Men must not walk too late." He
says nothing about Macbeth having killed Duncan and Banquo, but
he *means* that Macbeth has killed them.

and speeches is so pervasive, especially in *King Oedipus*, that **Sophoclean irony** has become a critical term. Here is a critic summarizing the ironies of *King Oedipus:*

> As the images unfold, the enquirer turns into the object of enquiry, the hunter into the prey, the doctor into the patient, the investigator into the criminal, the revealer into the thing revealed, the finder into the thing found, the savior into the thing saved ("I was saved, for some dreadful destiny"), the liberator into the thing released ("I released your feet from the bonds which pierced your ankles" says the Corinthian messenger), the accuser becomes the defendant, the ruler the subject, the teacher not only the pupil but also the object lesson, the example.
>
> Bernard Knox, "Sophocles' Oedipus," in *Tragic Themes in Western Literature*, ed. Cleanth Brooks (New Haven, 1955), pp. 10–11

Notice, by the way, the masterliness of this sentence; it is unusually long, but it does not ramble, it does not baffle, and it does not suggest a stuffy writer. The verb "turns" governs the first two-thirds; and after the second long parenthesis, when there is danger that the messenger's speech will cause the reader to forget the verb, the writer provides another verb, "becomes."

When the deed backfires, or has a reverse effect, we have what Aristotle called a **peripeteia**, or a **reversal**. When a character comes to perceive what has happened (Macbeth's "I have lived long enough: my way of life / Is fall'n into the sere, the yellow leaf"), he experiences (in Aristotle's language) an **anagnorisis** or **recognition**. In his analysis of drama Aristotle says that the tragic hero comes to grief through his **hamaratia,** a term sometimes translated as **tragic flaw** but perhaps better translated as **tragic error**. Thus, it is a great error for Othello to trust Iago and to strangle Desdemona, for Lear to give away his kingdom, and for Macbeth to decide to help fulfill the prophecies. If we hold to the translation "flaw," we begin to hunt for a fault in their characters; and we say, for instance, that Othello is gullible, Lear self-indulgent, Macbeth ambitious, or some such thing. In doing this, we may overlook their grandeur. To take a single example: Iago boasts he can dupe Othello because

> The Moor is of a free and open nature
> That thinks men honest that but seem to be so.

We ought to hesitate before we say that a man who trusts men because they seem to be honest has a flaw.

When writing about tragedy, probably the commonest essay is on the tragic hero. Too often the hero is judged mechanically: he must be noble, he must have a flaw, he must do a fearful deed, he must recognize his flaw, he must die. The previous paragraph suggests that Shakespeare's practice makes doubtful one of these matters, the flaw. A student might be similarly cautious about accepting the rest of the package unexamined. On the other hand, if "tragedy" is to have any meaning — any use as a term — it must have some agreed-upon attributes. An essay that seeks to determine whether or not a character is a tragic character ought at its outset to make clear its conception of tragedy and the degree of rigidity, or flexibility, with which it will interpret some or all of its categories. For example, it may indicate that although nobility is a *sine qua non*, nobility is not equivalent to high rank. A middle-class figure with certain mental or spiritual characteristics may, in such a view, be an acceptable tragic hero.

An essay closely related to the sort we have been talking about measures a character by some well-known theory of tragedy. For example, one can measure Willy Loman, in *Death of a Salesman*, against Miller's essays on tragedy or against Aristotle's remarks on tragedy. The organization of such an essay is usually not a problem: isolate the relevant aspects of the theoretical statement, and then examine the character to see if, point by point, he illustrates them. But remember that even if Willy Loman fulfills Arthur Miller's idea of a tragic figure, you need not accept him as tragic; conversely, if he does not fulfill Aristotle's idea, you need not deny him tragic status. Aristotle may be wrong.

In **comedy,** the fullest life is seen to reside within social norms: at the beginning of a comedy we find banished dukes, unhappy lovers, crabby parents, jealous husbands, and harsh laws; but at the end we usually have a unified and genial society, often symbolized by a marriage feast to which everyone, or almost everyone, is invited. Early in *A Midsummer Night's Dream*, for instance, we meet quarreling young lovers and a father who demands that his daughter either marry a man she does not love or enter a convent. Such is the Athenian law. At the end of the play the lovers are properly matched, to everyone's satisfaction.

Speaking broadly, most comedies fall into one of two classes, **satiric comedy** and **romantic comedy.** In the former, the em

phasis is on the obstructionists — the irate fathers, hardheaded business men, and other members of the Establishment who at the beginning of the play seem to hold all of the cards, preventing joy from reigning. They are held up to ridicule because they are monomaniacs enslaved to themselves, acting mechanistically (always irate, always hard-headed) instead of responding genially to the ups and downs of life. The outwitting of these obstructionists often provides the resolution to the plot. Jonson, Molière, and Shaw are in this tradition; their comedy, according to an ancient Roman formula, "chastens morals with ridicule." On the other hand, in romantic comedy (one thinks of Shakespeare's *A Midsummer Night's Dream, As You Like It,* and *Twelfth Night*) the emphasis is put on a world of delightful people who engage our sympathies as they run their obstacle race to the altar. There are obstructionists here too, but the emphasis is elsewhere.

Essays on comedy often examine the nature of the humor. Why is an irate father, in this particular context, funny? Or why is a young lover, again in this particular context, funny? Commonly one will find that at least some of the humor is in the disproportionate nature of their activities (they get terribly excited) and in their inflexibility. In both of these qualities they are rather like the cat in animated cartoons, who repeatedly chases the mouse to his hole and who repeatedly bangs his head against the wall. Suppose one wishes to write an essay on why Jaques in *As You Like It* is amusing. It might run something like this:

Jaques is insistently melancholy. In the Eden-like Forest of Arden, he sees only the dark side of things.

His monomania, however, is harmless to himself and to others; because it causes us no pain, it may entertain us.

Indeed, we begin to look forward to his melancholy speeches. We delight in hearing him fulfill our expectations by wittily finding gloom where others find mirth.

We are delighted, too, to learn that this chastizer of others has in fact been guilty of the sort of behavior he chastizes.

At the end of the play, when four couples are wed, the inflexible Jaques insists on standing apart from the general rejoicing.

Such might be the gist of an essay. It needs to be supported with details, and it can be enriched, for example, by a comparison between his sort of jesting and Touchstone's; but it is at least a promising draft of an outline.

Every play, of course, is different from every other play; each is a unique and detailed statement, and the previous paragraphs give only the broadest outlines — comedies and tragedies seen at a distance, as it were. The analyst's job is to try to study the differences as well as the similarities, in an effort (in Henry James's words) "to appreciate, to appropriate, to take intellectual possession, to establish in fine a relation with the criticized thing and make it one's own."

The best way to make a work of art one's own is (again in Henry James's words) "to be one of the people on whom nothing is lost." If we have perceived the work properly, we ought to be able to formulate its **theme,** its underlying idea. Some critics, it is true, have argued that the concept of theme is meaningless. They hold that *Macbeth*, for example, gives us only an extremely detailed history of one imaginary man. In this view, *Macbeth* says nothing to you or me; it only says what happened to some imaginary man. Even *Julius Caesar* says nothing about the historical Julius Caesar or about the nature of Roman politics. Here we can agree; no one would offer Shakespeare's play as evidence of what the historical Caesar said or did. But surely the view that the concept of theme is meaningless, and that a work tells us only about imaginary creatures, is a desperate one. We *can* say that we see in *Julius Caesar* the fall of power, or (if we are thinking of Brutus) the vulnerability of idealism, or some such things. To the reply that these are mere truisms, we can counter: Yes, but the truisms are presented in such a way that they take on life and become a part of us rather than remain things of which we say "I've heard it said, and I guess it's so." And surely we are in no danger of equating the play with the theme that we sense underlies it. We never believe that our statement of the theme is the equivalent of the play itself. We recognize that the play presents the theme with such detail that our statement is only a wedge to help us enter into the play so that we may more fully appropriate it. Joseph Wood Krutch discusses at some length the themes of *Death of a Salesman* and *A Streetcar Named Desire* on pp. 148–52, but a briefer illus-

tration may be helpful here. A critic examining Ibsen's achieve-
ments begins by trying to see what some of the plays are in fact
about.

> We must not waste more than a paragraph on such fiddle-faddle
> as the notion that *Ghosts* is a play about venereal disease or that
> *A Doll's House* is a play about women's rights. On these terms,
> *King Lear* is a play about housing for the elderly and *Hamlet* is a
> stage-debate over the reality of spooks. Venereal disease and its
> consequences are represented onstage in *Ghosts*; so, to all intents and
> purposes, is incest; but the theme of the play is inherited guilt, and
> the sexual pathology of the Alving family is an engine in the hands
> of that theme. *A Doll's House* represents a woman imbued with
> the idea of becoming a person, but it proposes nothing categorical
> about women becoming people; in fact, its real theme has nothing
> to do with the sexes. It is the irrepressible conflict of two different
> personalities which have founded themselves on two radically dif-
> ferent estimates of reality.
>
> > Robert M. Adams, "Ibsen on the Contrary," in *Modern
> > Drama*, ed. Anthony Caputi (New York, 1966), p. 345

Such a formulation can be most useful; a grasp of the theme
helps us to see what the plot is really all about, what the plot
suggests in its universal meaning or applicability.

A few words about the preceding quotation may be useful
here. Notice that Adams' paragraph moves from a vigorous
colloquial opening through some familiar examples, including a
brief comparison with plays by another dramatist, to a fairly
formal close. The disparity in tone between opening and closing
is not distressing because even in the opening we sense the
writer's mastery of his material, and we sympathize with his im-
patience. Adams' next paragraph, not given here, extends his
suggestion that the plays are not about nineteenth-century problems: he argues that under the bourgeois décor, under the frock
coat and the bustle, we detect two kinds of people — little people and great people. His third paragraph elaborates this point
by suggesting that, allowing for variations, the dichotomy consists of satyrs and saints, and he provides the details necessary
to make this dichotomy convincing. Among Ibsen's little people,
or satyrs, are Parson Manders, Peter Stockmann, Hialmar Ekdal,
and Torvald Helmer; among the great people, or saints, are
Mrs. Alving, Thomas Stockmann, Gregers Werle, and Nora

Helmer. In short, Adams' argument about Ibsen's themes advances steadily, and is convincingly illustrated with concrete references.

Although **action** commonly denotes physical movement, some critics (influenced by Aristotle's statement that a drama is an imitation of an action) use it in a sense equivalent to theme. In this sense, the action is the underlying happening — the inner happening — for example, "the enlightenment of a man" or "the coming of unhappiness to a man" or "the finding of the self by self-surrender." Francis Fergusson suggests that an expression in *Macbeth* to the effect that Macbeth "outran the pauser, reason" describes the action of the play. A paragraph from his chapter on *Macbeth* may clarify this conception:

> To "outrun" reason suggests an impossible stunt, like lifting oneself by one's own bootstraps. It also suggests a competition or race, like those of nightmare, which cannot be won. As for the word "reason," Shakespeare associates it with nature and nature's order, in the individual soul, in society, and in the cosmos. To outrun reason is thus to violate nature itself, to lose the bearings of common sense and of custom, and to move into a spiritual realm bounded by the irrational darkness of Hell one way, and the superrational grace of faith the other way. As the play develops before us, all the modes of this absurd, or evil, or supernatural, action are attempted, the last being Malcolm's and Macduff's acts of faith.
>
> *The Human Image in Dramatic Literature*
> (New York, 1957), p. 118

In this view, the dramatist conceives of an action and then imitates it or sets it forth by means of, first of all, a plot and characters, then by means of language, gesture, and perhaps spectacle and music. When the Greek comic dramatist Menander told a friend he had finished his play and now had only to write it, he must have meant that he had the action or the theme firmly in mind, and had worked out the plot and the requisite characters. All that remained was to set down the words.

Plot is variously defined, sometimes as equivalent to "story" (in this sense a synopsis of *Julius Caesar* has the same plot as *Julius Caesar*), but more often, and more usefully, as the dramatist's particular *arrangement of the story*. Thus, because Shakespeare's *Julius Caesar* begins with a scene dramatizing an encounter between plebeians and tribunes, its plot is different from that of a play on Julius Caesar in which such a scene (not necessary to the story) is omitted. Here is Richard G. Moulton, discussing the early part of Shakespeare's plot in *Julius Caesar*. He is examining the relationship between the first two scenes.

> The opening scene strikes appropriately the key-note of the whole action. In it we see the tribunes of the people — officers whose whole *raison d'être* is to be the mouthpiece of the commonalty — restraining their own clients from the noisy honors they are disposed to pay Caesar. To the justification in our eyes of a conspiracy against Caesar, there could not be a better starting-point than this hint that the popular worship of Caesar, which has made him what he is, is itself reaching its reaction-point. Such a suggestion moreover makes the whole play one complete *wave* of popular fickleness from crest to crest.
>
> The second is the scene upon which the dramatist mainly relies for the *crescendo* in the justification of the conspirators. It is a long scene, elaborately contrived so as to keep the conspirators and their cause before us at their very best, and the victim at his very worst.
> *Shakespeare as a Dramatic Artist* (Oxford, 1893), pp. 188–89

Moulton's discussion of the plot continues at length. One can argue that he presents too favorable a view of the conspirators (when he says we see the conspirators at their best he seems to overlook their fawning), but that is not our concern here; here we have been talking about the process of examining juxtaposed scenes, a process Moulton's words illustrate well. Handbooks on the drama often suggest that a plot (arrangement of happenings) should have a **rising action,** a **climax,** and a **falling action.** This sort of plot can be diagrammed as a pyramid, the tension rising through complications or **crises** to a climax, at which point the climax is the apex, and the tension allegedly slackens as we witness the **dénouement** (unknotting). Shakespeare sometimes used a pyramidal structure, placing his climax neatly in the middle of what seems to us to be the third of five acts. Roughly the first half of *Romeo and Juliet,* for example, shows Romeo winning Juliet; but when in III.i he kills her cousin Tybalt, Romeo sets in motion (it is often said) the second half of the play, the losing of Juliet and of his own life. Similarly, in *Julius Caesar,* Brutus rises in the first half of the play, reaching his height in III.i, with the death of Caesar; but later in this scene he gives Marc Antony permission to speak at Caesar's funeral, and thus he sets in motion his own fall, which occupies the second

half of the play. In *Macbeth*, the protagonist attains his height in
III.i ("Thou hast it now: King"), but he soon perceives that he
is going downhill:

> I am in blood
> Stepped in so far, that, should I wade no more,
> Returning were as tedious as go o'er.

In *Hamlet*, the protagonist proves to his own satisfaction
Claudius' guilt (by the play within the play) in III.ii, but almost
immediately he begins to worsen his position, by failing to kill
Claudius when he is an easy target (III.iii) and by contaminat-
ing himself with the murder of Polonius (III.iv).

There is, of course, no law that demands such a structure, and
a hunt for the pyramid usually causes the hunter to overlook all
the crises but the middle one. William Butler Yeats once sug-
gestively diagrammed a good plot not as a pyramid but as a line
moving diagonally upward, punctuated by several crises. Perhaps
it is sufficient to say that a good plot has its moments of tension,
but that the location of these will vary with the play. They are
the product of **conflict,** but it should be noted that not all conflict produces tension; there is conflict but no tension in a ball
game when the score is 10–0 and the visiting pitcher comes to
bat in the ninth inning with two out and none on base.

Regardless of how a plot is diagrammed, the **exposition** is
that part which tells the audience what it has to know about the
past, the **antecedent action.** Two gossiping servants who tell each
other that after a year away in Paris the young master is coming
home tomorrow with a new wife are giving the audience the
exposition. The exposition in Shakespeare's *The Tempest* is almost ruthlessly direct: Prospero tells his naïve daughter, "I
should inform thee farther," and for about one hundred and
fifty lines he proceeds to tell her why she is on an almost uninhabited island. Prospero's harangue is punctuated by his
daughter's professions of attention; but the Elizabethans (and
the Greeks) sometimes tossed out all pretense at dialogue, and
began with a **prologue,** like the one spoken by the Chorus at the
outset of *Romeo and Juliet:*

> Two households, both alike in dignity
>> In fair Verona, where we lay our scene,
> From ancient grudge break to new mutiny,
>> Where civil blood makes civil hands unclean.
> From forth the fatal loins of these two foes
>> A pair of star-crossed lovers take their life. . . .

On the other hand, the exposition may extend far into the play, being given in dribs and drabs.

Exposition has been discussed as though it simply consists of informing the audience about events; but exposition can do much more. It can give us an understanding of the characters who themselves are talking about other characters, it can evoke a mood, and it can generate tension. When we summarize the opening act, and treat it as "mere exposition," we are probably losing what is in fact dramatic in it. Moulton, in his analysis of the first two scenes in *Julius Caesar*, does not make the mistake of thinking that the first scenes exist merely to tell the audience certain facts.

An analysis of plot, then, will consider the arrangement of the episodes, the effect of juxtapositions, as well as the overall story. A useful essay can be written on the function of one scene. Such an essay may point out, for example, that the curious scene (IV.iii) in which Malcolm, Macduff, and Ross converse near the palace of the King of England serves to indicate that even good men must tell lies during Macbeth's reign, that Macbeth has the vile qualities that Malcolm pretends to have, and that Macbeth has failed — as the King of England has not — to be a source of health to the realm. Sometimes an analysis of plot will examine the relationships between the several stories in a play: *A Midsummer Night's Dream* has supernatural lovers, mature royal lovers, young Athenian lovers, a bumpkin who briefly becomes the lover of the fairy queen, and a play (put on by the bumpkins) about legendary lovers. How these are held together and how they help to define each other and the total play are matters that concern anyone looking at the plot of *A Midsummer Night's Dream*. Richard Moulton suggests that Shakespeare's subplots "have the effect of assisting the main stories, smoothing away their difficulties and making their prominent points yet more prominent." He demonstrates his thesis at some length, but a very brief extract from his discussion of the Jessica-Lorenzo story, in *The Merchant of Venice*, may be enough to suggest the method. The main story concerns Shylock and his rivals, Antonio, Bassanio, and Portia. Shylock's daughter Jessica is not needed for the narrative purpose of the main story. Why then did Shakespeare include her? Part of Moulton's answer runs thus:

> A Shylock painted without a tender side at all would be repulsive
> . . . and yet it appears how this tenderness has grown hard and

rotten with the general debasement of his soul by avarice, until, in his ravings over his loss, his ducats and his daughters are ranked as equally dear.

> I would my daughter were dead at my foot, and the jewels in her ear! Would she were hearsed at my foot, and the ducats in her coffin!

For all this we feel that he is hardly used in losing her. Paternal feeling may take a gross form, but it is paternal feeling none the less, and cannot be denied our sympathy; bereavement is a common ground upon which not only high and low, but even the pure and the outcast, are drawn together. Thus Jessica at home makes us hate Shylock; with Jessica lost we cannot help pitying him.

Shakespeare as a Dramatic Artist, p. 79

Before we proceed to talk about gestures, setting, and characterization, it may be useful to touch on dramatic **conventions**. An artist and his audience have some tacit — even unconscious — agreements. When we watch a motion picture and see an image dissolve and then reappear, we understand that some time has passed. Such an unrealistic, but widely accepted, device is a convention. In the theater, we sometimes see on the stage a room, realistic in all details except that it lacks a fourth wall; were that wall in place, we would see it and not the interior of the room. We do not regret the missing wall, and indeed we are scarcely aware that we have entered into an agreement to pretend that this strange room is an ordinary room with the usual number of walls. Sometimes the characters in a play speak verse, although outside of the theater no human beings speak verse for more than a few moments. Again we accept the device because it allows the author to make a play, and we want a play. In *Hamlet* the characters are understood to be speaking Danish, in *Julius Caesar* Latin, in *A Midsummer Night's Dream* Greek, yet they all speak English for our benefit. Two other conventions are especially common in older drama: the **soliloquy** and the **aside**. In the former, although a solitary character speaks his thoughts aloud, we do not judge him to be a lunatic; in the latter, a character speaks in the presence of others but is understood not to be heard by them, or to be heard only by those to whom he directs his words. The soliloquy and the aside strike us as artificial — and they are. But they so strike us only because they are no longer customary. Because we are accustomed to it, we are not bothered by the artificiality of music accompanying dialogue in a motion picture. The conventions of the modern theater are equally artificial but are so customary that we do not notice them. The Elizabethans, who saw a play acted without a break, would probably find strange our assumption that, when we return to the auditorium after a ten-minute intermission, the ensuing action may be supposed to follow immediately the action before the intermission.

The language of a play, broadly conceived, includes the **gestures** that the characters make and the **settings** in which they make them. As Ezra Pound somewhere says, "The medium of drama is not words, but persons moving about on a stage using words." When Shaw's Major Barbara, in a Salvation Army shelter, gives up the Army's insignia, pinning it on the collar of her millionaire father, who has, she says, bought the Army, the gesture is at least as important as the words that accompany it. Gesture can be interpreted even more broadly: the mere fact that a character enters, leaves, or does not enter may be highly significant. William Rosen (p. 143) calls attention to the way in which King Lear's

> formal entrance highlights all the dignity and authority associated with kingship. . . . On the Elizabethan stage this would be a stately procession of splendor, Lear the central figure in a crowded scene. All are Lear's subjects, dependent on him.

Here is John Russell Brown commenting on the actions and the absence of certain words that in *Hamlet* convey the growing separation between Gertrude and Claudius.

> Their first appearance together with a public celebration of marriage is a large and simple visual effect, and Gertrude's close concern for her son suggests a simple, and perhaps unremarkable modification . . . . But Claudius enters without Gertrude for his "Prayer Scene" (III.iii) and, for the first time, Gertrude enters without him for the Closet Scene (III.iv) and is left alone, again for the first time, when Polonius hides behind the arras. Thereafter earlier accord is revalued by an increasing separation, often poignantly silent, and unexpected. When Claudius calls Gertrude to leave with him after Hamlet has dragged off Polonius' body, she makes no reply; twice more he urges her and she is still silent. But he does not remonstrate or question; rather he speaks of his own immediate concerns and, far from supporting her with assurances, becomes more aware of his own fears:
>
> O, come away!
> My soul is full of discord and dismay.
> (IV.i.44–45)

Emotion has been so heightened that it is remarkable that they leave together without further words. The audience has been aware of a new distance between Gertrude and Claudius, of her immobility and silence, and of his self-concern, haste and insistence.

Shakespeare's Plays in Performance (New York, 1967), p. 139

Sometimes the dramatist helps us to interpret the gestures; Shaw and O'Neill give notably full stage directions, but detailed stage directions before the middle of the nineteenth century are rare.

Drama of the nineteenth and early twentieth century is often thought to be "realistic," but of course even a realistic play-wright or stage designer selects his materials. A realistic setting (indication of the locale), then, can say a great deal, can serve as a symbol. Here is Ibsen on nonverbal devices:

I can do quite a lot by manipulating the prosaic details of my plays so that they become theatrical metaphors and come to mean more than what they are; I have used costume in this way, lighting, scenery, landscape, weather; I have used trivial everyday things like inky fingers and candles; and I have used living figures as symbols of spiritual forces that act upon the hero. Perhaps these things could be brought into the context of a modern realistic play to help me to portray the modern hero and the tragic conflict which I now understand so well.

Quoted by John Northam, "Ibsen's Search for the Hero," in *Ibsen*, ed. Rolf Fjelde (Englewood Cliffs, N.J., 1965), p. 99

To take two of Ibsen's suggestive details in the setting of *Hedda Gabler*: early in the play Hedda is distressed by the sunlight that shines through the opened French doors, a detail that we later see helps to reveal her fear of the processes of nature. More evident and more pervasive is her tendency, when she cannot cope with her present situation, to move to the inner room, at the rear of the stage, in which hangs a picture of her late father.

Contemporary dramatists are often explicit about the symbolic qualities of the setting. Here are two examples, the first from O'Neill's *Desire under the Elms*, the second from Miller's *Death of a Salesman*. In both examples only a part of the initial stage direction is given:

The house is in good condition but in need of paint. Its walls are a sickly grayish, the green of the shutters faded. Two enormous elms are on each side of the house. They bend their trailing branches down over the roof. They appear to protect and at the same time subdue. There is a sinister maternity in their aspect, a crushing, jealous absorption . . . . They are like exhausted women resting their sagging breasts and hands and hair on its roof . . . .

And now Miller's description of the set in *Death of a Salesman:*

Before us is the Salesman's house. We are aware of towering, angular shapes behind it, surrounding it on all sides. Only the blue light of the sky falls upon the house and forestage; the surrounding area shows an angry glow of orange. As more light appears, we see a solid vault of apartment houses around the small, fragile-seeming home.

These directions and the settings they describe are symbols that help to give the plays their meaning. Not surprisingly, O'Neill's play has Freudian overtones, Miller's (in a broad sense) Marxist overtones. O'Neill is concerned about passion, Miller (note the "solid vault of apartment houses" that menaces the salesman's house) about social forces that warp the individual. An essay might examine in detail the degree to which the setting contributes to the theme of the play. Take, for example, O'Neill's setting. The maternal elms are the most important aspect, but an essayist might first point out that the "good condition" of the house suggests it was well built, presumably some years ago. The need of paint, however, suggests both present neglect and indifference to decoration, and indeed the play is partly concerned with a strong, miserly father who regards his sons as decadent. The house, "a sickly grayish," helps to embody the suggestion of old strength but present decadence. One might continue through the stage direction, explaining the relevance of the details. Contrasts between successive settings can be especially important.

Because Shakespeare's plays were performed in broad daylight on a stage that (compared with Ibsen's, O'Neill's, and Miller's) made little use of scenery, he had to use language to manufacture his settings. But the attentive ear, or the mind's eye, responds to these settings too. Early in *King Lear*, for example, when Lear reigns, we hear that we are in a country "With plenteous rivers, and wide-skirted meads"; later, when Lear is stripped of his power, we are in a place where "For many miles about / There's scarce a bush." (Incidentally, the vogue for the relatively bare stage which has been with us for a couple of decades is not merely an attempt to clear the stage of unnecessary furniture; in many plays it functions as a symbol of man's barren existence or of his existential plight. That is, the very sparseness of the decor or the black backdrop says something about the people who move on the stage.)

Characterization, or personality, is defined by what the characters do (a stage direction tells us that "Hedda paces up and down, clenching her fists"), by what they say (she asks her husband to draw the curtains), and by the setting in which they move. The characters are also defined in part by other characters whom they in some degree resemble. Hamlet, Laertes, and Fortinbras have each lost their fathers, but Hamlet spares the praying King Claudius, whereas Laertes, seeking vengeance on Hamlet for murdering Laertes' father, says he would cut Hamlet's throat in church; Hamlet meditates about the nature of action, but Fortinbras leads the Norwegians in a military campaign and ultimately acquires Denmark. Here is Kenneth Muir commenting briefly on the way in which Laertes helps us to see Hamlet more precisely. (Notice how Muir first offers a generalization, then supports it with details, and finally offers an even more important generalization that effectively closes his paragraph.)

> In spite of Hamlet's description of him as "a very noble youth," there is a coarseness of fibre in Laertes which is revealed throughout the play. He has the stock responses of a man of his time and position. He gives his sister copy-book advice; he goes to Paris (we are bound to suspect) to tread the primrose path; and after his father's death and again at his sister's grave he shows by the ostentation and "bravery of his grief" that he pretends more than he really feels. He has no difficulty in raising a successful rebellion against Claudius, which suggests that the more popular prince could have done the same. Laertes, indeed, acts more or less in the way that many critics profess to think Hamlet ought to act; and his function in the play is to show precisely the opposite. Although Hamlet himself may envy Laertes' capacity for ruthless action we ought surely to prefer Hamlet's craven scruples.
>
> *Shakespeare: The Great Tragedies* (London, 1961), pp. 12–13

Other plays, of course, provide examples of such **foils,** or characters who set one another off. Macbeth and Banquo both hear prophecies, but they act and react differently; Brutus is one kind of assassin, Cassius another, and Casca still another. Any analysis of a character, then, will probably have to take into

account, in some degree, the other characters that help to show
what he is, that help to set forth his **motivation** (grounds for
action, inner drives, goals). Here is a critic's discussion of the
part Dr. Rank, in Ibsen's A *Doll's House*, plays in helping to
define Nora:

> This is not Rank's play, it is Nora's. Rank is a minor character —
> but he plays a vital dramatic role. His function is to act as the
> physical embodiment, visible on the stage, of Nora's moral situation
> as she sees it. Nora is almost hysterical with terror at the thought of
> her situation — almost, but it is part of her character that with great
> heroism she keeps her fears secret to herself; and it is because of her
> reticence that Rank is dramatically necessary, to symbolize the horror
> she will not talk about. Nora feels, and we feel, the full awfulness
> of Rank's illness, and she transfers to herself the same feeling about
> the moral corruption which she imagines herself to carry. Nora sees
> herself, and we see her seeing herself (with our judgment), as suf-
> fering from a moral disease as mortal, as irremediable as Rank's
> disease, a disease that creeps on to a fatal climax. This is the foe
> that Nora is fighting so courageously.
>
> John Northam, "Ibsen's Search for the Hero," p. 103

Finally, a warning about character: in most drama, every
character is a more or less unreliable spokesman. What he says is
conditioned by his personality and by the people to whom he is
speaking. (An exception: One can assume that when a character
soliloquizes he is telling the truth as he sees it; at such a moment there is no one on whom he is trying to make an impression.) Suppose, for example, we look at Claudius' speech telling
Hamlet that Hamlet's grief for his father is excessive.

> 'Tis sweet and commendable in your nature, Hamlet,
> To give these mourning duties to your father,
> But you must know your father lost a father,
> That father lost, lost his, and the survivor bound
> In filial obligation for some term
> To do obsequious sorrow. But to persever
> In obstinate condolement is a course
> Of impious stubbornness. 'Tis unmanly grief.
> It shows a will most incorrect to heaven,
> A heart unfortified, a mind impatient,
> An understanding simple and unschooled.
> For what we know must be and is as common
> As any the most vulgar thing to sense,
> Why should we in our peevish opposition

Take it to heart? Fie, 'tis a fault to heaven,
A fault against the dead, a fault to nature,
To reason most absurd, whose common theme
Is death of fathers, and who still hath cried,
From the first corse till he that died today,
"This must be so." We pray you throw to earth
This unprevailing woe, and think of us
As of a father, for let the world take note
You are the most immediate to our throne,
And with no less nobility of love
Than that which dearest father bears his son
Do I impart toward you. For your intent
In going back to school in Wittenberg,
It is most retrograde to our desire,
And we beseech you, bend you to remain
Here in the cheer and comfort of our eye,
Our chiefest courtier, cousin, and our son.   (I.ii.87–117)

What can one write about this speech? Out of context, it is
reasonable enough; and certainly the point that everyone's father
dies is unexceptionable. But the speech exists within a context.
We have earlier seen the ghost of the late king, and Horatio
had suggested that ghosts walked "a little ere the mightiest
Julius fell," thus implanting in our minds the possibility that
the ghost in *Hamlet* too is somehow related to an assassination.
(The relation is twofold: King Hamlet was assassinated, and
Claudius, his successor, will be assassinated at the end of the
play.) Moreover, Hamlet's wry comments (in the speech preceding the quotation) about "the fruitful river in the eye" and
other highly visible manifestations of sorrow serve to diminish
Claudius' easy oratory. Most important, we notice, on rereading
the scene after we have read the entire play and learned that
Claudius murdered his brother, that Claudius, in the quoted
speech, accuses Hamlet of impiety. In fact, it is Claudius, and
not Hamlet, who has committed "a fault to heaven, / A fault
against the dead, a fault to nature," and the odiousness of this
fault is emphasized by Claudius' own pat reference to "the first
corse" (corpse), for this first corpse was that of Abel, killed by
his brother, as King Hamlet was killed by his brother. One might
notice, too, Claudius' insistence that Hamlet remain in Denmark, where Claudius can keep an eye on him, though a few
moments earlier Claudius had granted Laertes leave to return to
Paris. In short, a speech that seems plausible and even pious is

the utterance of a murderer who daringly (or guiltily?) glances at his own crime in the reference to Abel, who cunningly suggests that his opponent is sinful, and who virtually imprisons his opponent under the guise of offering fatherly comfort. Charles Lamb has a comment relevant to this point that one must consider the context: "Everything, in heaven and earth, in man and in story, in books and in fancy, acts by confederacy, by juxtaposition, by circumstance and place."

CONCLUDING REMARKS
ON WRITING ABOUT DRAMA

In writing about drama, most of us are likely to pay most of our attention to the words on the page, an understandable procedure if we regard drama as literature. Probably the great majority of essays are about the characterization of So-and-so. These essays usually look at a character's words, actions, and the setting in which he moves, as well as at what others say about him and do to him. With a play of great complexity, for example, one of Shakespeare's major plays, a short essay may do well to take an even smaller topic, such as Iago's use of prose (Why does he sometimes speak in prose, sometimes in verse, and what does it tell us about him?) or Hamlet's bawdy talk (Why does this prince sometimes make off-color remarks?). Even here we will not be able merely to hunt through the play looking at Iago's prose or Hamlet's bawdry; we will have to pay some attention to other usages of prose in *Othello*, or to other jesting in *Hamlet*, if we are to see the exact nature of the problem we have chosen to isolate.

But words are not, it has been argued above, the only language of drama, and a student will sometimes want to explore matters of staging. What is especially difficult, for most of us confronted with only a printed page, is to catch the full dramatic quality of a play — to read the words and also to have a sense of how they will sound in the context of gestures and a setting. We tend to read drama as literature rather than as dramatic literature, or theater. When the author is Shakespeare or Shaw, we can sometimes justly examine his works as literature, although even here we may find that things that seem flat on the page come alive in the theater. (Those unfunny clowns in Shakespeare are usually performed today by minor actors on the assumption that the parts are of no value; when cast well — in Shakespeare's day some of the best-known actors were those who played the clowns — these parts of the play take on meaning.) Of the two essays on drama included in this book, William Rosen's is the more theatrical. Joseph Wood Krutch discusses the themes of *Death of a Salesman* and of *A Streetcar Named Desire*, with a glance at the tradition of tragic literature. Rosen tries to see how we perceive King Lear during the first scene. Both methods can be fruitful.

5

POETRY

Aristotle suggested that the arts arise out of two impulses: the impulse for harmony and the impulse to imitate. Let us take these one at a time.

We are all familiar with the desire to make a pattern. We straighten pictures on the walls (we like parallel lines), and we arrange the silverware on the table in a way that pleases. (Even chimpanzees are said to show what is called an instinct for closure. If they are given paint and a brush and a paper on which two-thirds of a circle has been painted, they will sometimes complete the circle.) We make patterns too out of sounds; if we forget a line of a song, we do not leave an unpleasant blank, but we feel compelled to fill it out by humming or by uttering nonsense syllables such as *da da da da da*. Sometimes the sounds make a sort of sense, but the sense scarcely seems important. The following lines have pleased for generations, presumably because of their catchiness rather than because of any message.

Pease-porridge hot,
    Pease-porridge cold,
Pease-porridge in the pot
    Nine days old.

Something about meter, rhythm, and rhyme will be said below, but for the moment we can say that one source of pleasure in poetry is afforded by its harmonious pattern of sounds.

The meaning affords a second source of pleasure. Poetry is sound and sense, and in this connection we may briefly consider Aristotle's statement that the second psychological impulse behind the arts is the impulse to imitate. Children mimicking their parents or playing cops and robbers provide examples of the impulse to imitate. And it is easy to see that a landscape painting is a sort of imitation (in pigment) of a landscape; a piece of sculpture is an imitation (in wood or stone) of, say, Moses; a historical novel is an imitation (in words) of some aspect of a period of time; a play is an imitation (in words and gestures) of the doings of men. Because in ordinary language, however, "imitation" has a pejorative overtone, the idea may become more acceptable if we substitute "representation" or "re-creation." Now, this representation is not an exact duplicate; as the previous chapter mentioned, no one believes that *Julius Caesar* is a mirror image of what happened in Rome two thousand years ago. Shakespeare took some hints from history (a leader assassinated), but he invented speeches and even some characters. And his *Julius Caesar* offers itself as a coherent and meaningful work; Caesar may never have said this or done that, but Shakespeare's words combine to give us an imitation that helps us to see the invisible relationships in our own world, somewhat as a mimic of X suddenly — by heightening certain features of X's gestures and intonations — makes us see and hear things we had not before noticed in X. Through the imitation, we perceive, let us say, the insecurity that underlies X's words and gestures. But this is to speak of drama and impersonation, not specifically of poetry. In what sense is nondramatic poetry an imitation? And let us make the problem more difficult by eliminating such narratives as *The Odyssey* and *Paradise Lost*, for clearly they imitate — that is, they present in words — actions that allegedly happened long ago. Let us talk at first about what is commonly called lyric poetry.

The **lyric** commonly presents a speaker expressing an emotion. The name suggests that it was once a song to be accompanied by a lyre, and although the genre now includes much that cannot possibly be sung, let us begin with the singable.

ROBERT BURNS

Auld Lang Syne°   *long ago*

Should auld acquaintance be forgot,
    And never brought to mind?
Should auld acquaintance be forgot,
    And auld lang syne!

    For auld lang syne, my jo,
        For auld lang syne,
    We'll tak a cup o' kindness yet
        For auld lang syne.

And surely ye'll be your pint-stowp!°   *pay for your pint-cup*
    And surely I'll be mine!
And we'll tak a cup o' kindness yet
    For auld lang syne.

We twa hae run about the braes,°   *slopes*
    And pu'd the gowans° fine;   *daisies*
But we've wander'd mony a weary fitt
    Sin auld lang syne.

We twa hae paidl'd i' the burn,°   *brook*
    From morning sun till dine;°   *dinner, noon*
But seas between us braid hae roar'd,
    Sin auld lang syne.

And there's a hand, my trusty fiere!°   *friend*
    And gie's a hand o' thine!
And we'll tak a right guid-willie-waught,°   *hearty swig*
    For auld lang syne.

It is not stretching a point to say that Burns's song imitates, or re-creates, a state that we all know in some degree. There are moments of conviviality that are suffused with a sense of the irrevocable past. This last sentence is an inept summary of the poem, but it affords a prologue to a simple question that may clarify the point: Do we not — and do not innumerable people who sing "Auld Lang Syne" on New Year's Eve — feel that Burns has perfectly caught, or imitated, a state of mind? Is not "Auld Lang Syne" an embodiment or imitation of a human experience? We value its sound (we may not even know the meanings of some of the words), and we also value its sense, the representation of a moment of human behavior. We hear a voice that is not at all literally like any voice we have ever heard (no

one talks in rhymes) but that nevertheless makes us say, "Yes,
I understand that experience. I see what that state of mind is."

Here is another voice, very far from a singing one:

ALEXANDER POPE

from *An Essay on Man*

Awake, my St. John!° leave all meaner things   *Henry St. John*
To low ambition, and the pride of kings.
Let us (since life can little more supply
Than just to look about us and to die)
Expatiate free o'er all this scene of Man;
A mighty maze! but not without a plan;
A wild, where weeds and flowers promiscuous shoot,
Or garden, tempting with forbidden fruit.
Together let us beat this ample field,
Try what the open, what the covert yield;
The latent tracts, the giddy heights, explore
Of all who blindly creep, or sightless soar;
Eye nature's walks, shoot folly as it flies,
And catch the manners living as they rise;
Laugh where we must, be candid where we can,
But vindicate the ways of God to man.

This poem proceeds for hundreds of lines, and we may not feel
that Pope vindicates the ways of God to man, but again we catch
a human voice. It begins authoritatively ("Awake") and yet
jocosely (low things, it says, are the concern of kings). Then,
in the third and fourth lines, a touch — but a highly controlled
touch — of pathos is introduced in the parenthetic reference to
the brevity of man's life. Next, the speaker suggests that the
world is a sort of large estate harboring all sorts of creatures. He
almost seems supercilious in his reference to shooting down folly
(i.e., some people are compared to stupid game birds), but his
good-natured "Laugh where we must, be candid [i.e., generous]
where we can" reminds us of the traditional and reasonable view
that wrongdoing appears funny (because it is self-defeating) to
the good man. We continue to listen with interest to this speaker
who, in the last line of this verse paragraph, reaffirms his high
purpose with an echo from Milton's *Paradise Lost*. What we have
is a man talking easily and intimately about something important.
We read Pope's *Essay on Man*, looking out both for the "ideas"
he sets forth, which may or may not prove convincing, and for

the voice or mind or personality, that is, for an imitation of a man thinking.

The **voice**, or **persona** (Latin for mask), or **mask**, that speaks the poem is not, of course, identical with the poet who writes it. The author counterfeits the speech of a person in a particular situation. Robert Browning, for example, invented a Renaissance duke who speaks "My Last Duchess"; Robert Frost in "Stopping by Woods on a Snowy Evening" invented the speech of a man who, sitting in a horse-drawn sleigh, is surveying woods that are "lovely, dark and deep."

The speaker's voice, of course, often has the ring of the author's own voice, and to make a distinction between speaker and author may at times seem perverse. Robert Burns, for example, sometimes lets us know that the poem is spoken by "Rob"; he may address his wife by name; beneath the title "To a Mouse" he writes, "On Turning Up Her Nest with the Plow, November, 1785," and beneath the title "To a Mountain Daisy" he writes, "On Turning One Down with the Plow in April, 1786." Still, even in these allegedly autobiographical poems, it may be convenient to distinguish between author and speaker; the speaker is Burns the lover, or Burns the meditative man, or Burns the compassionate man, not simply Robert Burns the poet.

The voice is established not only by broad strokes but by such details as **alliteration** (the repetition of initial consonants), **assonance** (the repetition of vowel-sounds), and rhyme. (More will be said about rhyme later.) F. W. Bateson, in *English Poetry*, aptly notes the role that alliteration plays in reinforcing the contemptuous tone we hear in "Die and endow a college or a cat," a line from Pope's "Epistle to Bathurst." Bateson points out that "the *d*'s hint that there is a subtle identity in the dying and the endowing (the only interest that the world takes in this particular death is in the testamentary endowments), and the *c*'s point the contrast between founding colleges and financing cats' homes."

From the whole of language, one consciously or unconsciously selects certain words and grammatical constructions; this selection constitutes one's **diction**. It is partly by the diction that we come to know the speaker of a poem. "Auld" and "twa" tell us that the speaker of "Auld Lang Syne" is a Scot. In the passage from Pope's *Essay on Man*, "expatiate," "promiscuous," and "vindicate" tell us that the speaker is an educated man. Of course, some words are used in both poems: "my," "to," "and." The fact remains, however, that although a large part of language is shared by all speakers, some parts of language are used only by certain speakers.

Like some words, some grammatical constructions are used only by certain kinds of speakers. Consider these two passages:

> In Adam's fall
> We sinned all.   (from *The New England Primer*)

> Of Man's first disobedience, and the fruit
> Of that forbidden tree whose mortal taste
> Brought death into the World, and all our woe,
> With loss of Eden, till one greater Man
> Restore us, and regain the blissful seat,
> Sing, Heavenly Muse, that, on the secret top
> Of Oreb, or of Sinai, didst inspire
> That shepherd who first taught the chosen seed
> In the beginning how the heavens and earth
> Rose out of Chaos. . . .   (Milton, from *Paradise Lost*)

There is an enormous difference in the diction of these two passages. Milton, speaking as an inspired poet who regards his theme as "a great argument," appropriately uses words and grammatical constructions somewhat removed from common life. Hence, while the anonymous author of the primer speaks directly of "Adam's fall," Milton speaks allusively of the fall, calling it "Man's first disobedience." Milton's sentence is nothing that any Englishman ever said in conversation; its genitive beginning, its length (the sentence continues for six lines beyond the quoted passage), and its postponement of the main verb until the sixth line mark it as the utterance of a poet working in the tradition of Latin poetry. The primer's statement, by its choice of words as well as by its brevity, suggests a far less sophisticated speaker.

A speaker (or voice, to use the previous terminology) has attitudes toward himself, his subject, and his audience, and (consciously or unconsciously) he chooses his words, pitch, and modulation accordingly; all these add up to his **tone.** In written literature, tone must be detected without the aid of the ear; the reader must understand by the selection and sequence of words the way (i.e., playfully, angrily, confidentially, ironically, etc.) in which they are meant to be heard. The reader must catch what

Frost calls "the speaking tone of voice somehow entangled in the words and fastened to the page for the ear of the imagination."[1]

Our interest in the shifting tones in the voice that speaks the words should not, of course, cause us to neglect the words themselves, the gist of the idea expressed. If we **paraphrase** (reword) the first two lines of Pope's *Essay on Man*, we get something like this: "Wake up, my friend St. John [the man addressed was Henry St. John], leave low things to such lowly people as are ambitious and (equally low) to arrogant monarchs." A paraphrase at least has the virtue of making us look hard at all of the words. In paraphrasing Pope, for example, we come to see that "my" in the first line reveals the intimacy which Pope feels toward St. John. If you paraphrase the next six lines of Pope's *Essay*, and then closely compare your paraphrase with Pope's words, you are doing some of the homework preliminary to writing an explication (see pp. 7–9) of the lines. To take the most obvious example: You will probably be able to see the implication that is in Pope's "garden, tempting with forbidden fruit." You may need a dictionary to see the multiple meanings in "Expatiate" and "promiscuous." But the point of a paraphrase is not to enlarge your vocabulary; it is an exercise designed to help you understand at least the surface meaning, and it will usually help you to understand at least some of the implicit meaning. Furthermore, a paraphrase makes you see that the poet's words — if the poem is a good one — are exactly right, better than the words you might substitute. It becomes clear that the thing said in the poem — not only the "idea" expressed but the precise tone with which it is expressed — is a sharply defined experience.

Let us consider now an anonymous quatrain, written in England about 1500.

Western wind, when wilt thou blow,
The small rain down can rain?
Christ, if my love were in my arms,
And I in my bed again.

This poem defies paraphrase, not because it is obscure or nonsensical, but because the surface statement is so lucid. The most

[1] This discussion concentrates on the speaker's tone. But sometimes one can also talk of the author's tone, that is, of the author's attitude toward his invented speaker. The speaker's tone might, for example, be angry, but the author's tone (as detected by the reader) might be humorous.

one can do in paraphrasing the first line is to say something like "O west wind [the opening is vocative, the wind is being addressed], when will you come?" About the only distortion from ordinary language in the poem is "small rain," where we would normally speak of the "light rain" or "gentle rain." But an explication will point out that much more is going on in the poem than a word-for-word substitution can indicate. The first two lines indicate that the speaker longs for the spring — the time of light rain and the time when the west wind (warmed by the Gulf Stream) blows in England. In the next two lines he expresses his unhappiness that he is not with his beloved. What is the connection between the first two and the last two lines? Among the answers are these: spring is commonly associated with lovers; spring is a time of warmth and revitalization, and love is associated with warmth and with new birth. The first two lines implicitly tell us it is winter, and the lover in effect compares the world's wintry state with his own wintriness (sense of coldness, barrenness) caused by the absence of his beloved. "Christ" in the third line may be both an agonized expletive and an invocation: he calls on Christ, who Himself was reborn in the spring (the Resurrection), and who is the giver of new life to men who sense the emptiness of their present lives. The previous sentences are tiresomely wordy (about a hundred words in place of the poem's twenty-six), but perhaps they help to illuminate the highly complex experience that we overhear in these four lines. Again, it is an experience that we are overhearing or witnessing, not an edifying message that we are receiving. The poem does not offer any answers to the questions: How shall I live? How can I regain the lover I have lost? It does, however, in memorable words, so perfectly catch a human experience that we feel the experience is available for us to look at, in contrast to our own daily experiences which are so much a welter that we can scarcely know them. In the preface to his *Collected Poems* Robert Frost, somewhat cryptically and punningly, talks about these matters of sound and sense and the knowledge of life that they afford:

> The sound is the gold in the ore. Then we will have the sound out alone and dispense with the inessential. We do till we make the discovery that the object in writing poetry is to make all poems sound as different as possible from each other, and the resources for that of vowels, consonants, punctuation, syntax, words, sentences, meter are not enough. We need the help of context — meaning — subject matter . . . . The possibilities for tune from the dramatic

tones of meaning struck across the rigidity of a limited meter are endless, and we are back in poetry as merely one more art of having something to say, sound or unsound. Probably better if sound, because deeper and from wider experience . . . . [A poem] begins in delight and ends in wisdom . . . a clarification of life — not necessarily a great clarification, such as sects and cults are founded on, but in a momentary stay against confusion . . . . For me the initial delight is in the surprise of remembering something I didn't know I knew. I am in a place, a situation, as if I had materialized from cloud or risen out of the ground.

Robert Frost has said, "Poetry provides the one permissible way of saying one thing and meaning another." This, of course, is an exaggeration, but it shrewdly suggests the importance of **figurative language** — saying one thing in terms of something else. Words have their literal meaning, but they can also be used so that something other than the literal meaning is implied. "My love is a rose" is, literally, nonsense, for she is not a five-petaled, many-stamened plant with a spiny stem. But the suggestions of "rose" include "delicate beauty," "soft," "perfumed," and thus the word "rose" can be meaningfully applied — figuratively rather than literally — to "my love." The girl is fragrant; her skin is perhaps like a rose in texture and (in some measure) color; she will not keep her beauty long. The poet, that is, has communicated a perception very precisely. His discovery is not world-shaking; it is less important than the discovery of America or the discovery that the meek are blessed, but it *is* a discovery and it offers that "clarification" and "momentary stay against confusion" that Frost spoke of.

People who write about poetry have found it convenient to name the various kinds of figurative language. Just as the student of geology employs special terms, such as kames and eskers, the student of literature employs special terms to name things as accurately as possible. The next few pages give the most common terms.

In a **simile** items from different classes are explicitly compared by a connective such as "like," "as," or "than," or by a verb such as "appears" or "seems." (If the objects compared are from the same class, e.g., "New York is like London," no simile is present.)

How like a marriage is the season of clouds.   (James Merrill)

It is a beauteous evening, calm and free.
The holy time is quiet as a Nun,
Breathless with adoration.   (Wordsworth)

How sharper than a serpent's tooth it is
To have a thankless child.   (Shakespeare)
Seems he a dove? His feathers are but borrowed.   (Shakespeare)

A **metaphor** asserts the identity, without a connective such as
"like" or a verb such as "appears," of terms that are literally
incompatible.

She is the rose, the glory of the day.   (Spenser)
O western orb sailing the heaven.   (Whitman)

Notice how in the last example only one of the terms ("orb") is
stated; the other ("ship") is implied in "sailing." In the following poem, Keat's excitement on reading Chapman's translation
of Homer is communicated first through a metaphor and then
through a simile.

JOHN KEATS

On First Looking into Chapman's Homer

Much have I traveled in the realms of gold,
And many goodly states and kingdoms seen;
Round many western islands have I been
Which bards in fealty to Apollo hold.
Oft of one wide expanse have I been told   5
That deep-browed Homer ruled as his demesne;
Yet did I never breathe its pure serene
Till I heard Chapman speak out loud and bold:

Then felt I like some watcher of the skies
When a new planet swims into his ken;   10
Or like stout Cortez when with eagle eyes
He stared at the Pacific — and all his men
Looked at each other with a wild surmise —
Silent, upon a peak in Darien.

We might pause for a moment to take a closer look at Keats's
poem. If we are asked to write an essay on the figurative language
in this sonnet, we will want to discuss the figure involved in
asserting that reading is a sort of traveling (it brings us to un-
familiar worlds), and especially that reading brings us to realms of
gold. Presumably the experience of reading is valuable. "Realms
of gold" not only continues and modifies the idea of reading as
travel, but in its evocation of El Dorado (an imaginary country

in South America, thought to be rich in gold and therefore the object of search by Spanish explorers of the Renaissance) it introduces a suggestion of the Renaissance appropriate to a poem about a Renaissance translation of Homer. The figure of traveling is amplified in the next few lines, which assert that the "goodly states and kingdoms" and "western islands" are ruled by poets who owe allegiance to a higher authority, Apollo. The beginning of the second sentence (line 5) enlarges this already spacious area with its reference to "one wide expanse," and the ruler of this area (unlike the other rulers) is given the dignity of being named. He is Homer, "deep-browed," "deep" suggesting not only his high, or perhaps furrowed, forehead but the profundity of the thoughts behind the forehead. The speaker continues the idea of books as remote places, but now he also seems to think of this place as more than a rich area; instead of merely saying that until he read Chapman's translation he had not "seen" it (as in line 2) or "been" there (line 3), he says he never breathed its air. The preciousness, that is, is not material but ethereal, not gold but something far more exhilarating and essential. This reference to air leads easily to the next dominant image, that of the explorer of the illimitable skies (so vast is Homer's world) rather than of the land and sea. But the explorer of the skies is conceived as watching an *oceanic* sky. In hindsight we can see that the link was perhaps forged earlier in line 7, with "serene" (a vast expanse of air *or* water); in any case, there is an unforgettable rightness in the description of the suddenly discovered planet as something that seems to "swim" into one's ken. After this climactic discovery we return to the Renaissance Spanish explorers (though, in fact, Balboa, and not Cortez, was the discoverer of the Pacific) by means of a simile that compares the speaker's rapture with Cortez's as he gazed at the expanse before him. The writer of an essay on the figurative language in a poem should, in short, try to call attention to the aptness (or ineptness) of the figures and to the connecting threads that make a meaningful pattern.

To continue with some basic terminology: two types of metaphor deserve special mention. In **synecdoche** the whole is replaced by the part, or the part by the whole. For example, "bread," in "Give us this day our daily bread," replaces the whole class of edibles. In **metonymy** something is named that replaces something closely related to it. For example, James Shirley names certain objects, using them to replace social classes to which they are related:

> Scepter and crown must tumble down
> And in the dust be equal made
> With the poor crooked scythe and spade

The attribution of human feelings or characteristics to abstractions or to inanimate objects is called **personification.**

> But Time did beckon to the flowers, and they
> By noon most cunningly did steal away.   (Herbert)

Herbert attributes a human gesture to Time and shrewdness to flowers. Of all figures, personification most surely gives to airy nothings a local habitation and a name:

> There's Wrath who has learnt every trick of guerilla warfare,
> The shamming dead, the night-raid, the feinted retreat.   (Auden)

> Hope, thou bold taster of delight.   (Crashaw)

Crashaw's personification, "Hope, thou bold taster of delight," is also an example of the figure called **apostrophe,** an address to a person or thing not literally listening. Wordsworth begins a sonnet by apostrophizing Milton:

> Milton, thou shouldst be living at this hour,

and Shelly begins an ode by apostrophizing a skylark:

> Hail to thee, blithe Spirit!

What conclusions can we draw about figurative language? Firstly, figurative language, with its literally incompatible terms, forces the reader to attend to the connotations (suggestions, associations) rather than to the denotations (dictionary definitions) of one of the terms. Secondly, although figurative language is said to differ from ordinary discourse, it is found in ordinary discourse as well as in literature. "It rained cats and dogs," "War is hell," "Don't be a pig," "Mr. Know-all," and other tired figures comprise part of our daily utterances. But through repeated use, these, and most of the figures we use, have lost whatever impact they once had and are only a shade removed from expressions which, though once figurative, have become literal: the *eye* of a needle, a *branch* office, the *face* of a clock. Thirdly, good figurative language is usually concrete, condensed, and interesting. The concreteness lends precision and vividness; when Keats writes that he felt "like some watcher of the skies / When a new planet swims into his ken," he more sharply characterizes his feelings than if he had said, "I felt excited." His simile isolates for us a precise kind of excitement, and the metaphoric "swims" vividly brings up the oceanic aspect of the sky. The second of these three qualities, condensation, can be seen by attempting to paraphrase some of the figures. A paraphrase will commonly use more words than the original, and it will have less impact — as the gradual coming of night usually has less impact on us than a sudden darkening of the sky, or as a prolonged push has less impact than a sudden blow. The third quality, interest, is largely dependent on the previous two: the successful figure often makes us open our eyes wider and take notice. Keats's "deep-browed Homer" arouses our interest in Homer as "thoughtful Homer" or "meditative Homer" does not. Similarly, when W. B. Yeats says:

> An aged man is but a paltry thing,
> A tattered coat upon a stick, unless
> Soul clap its hands and sing, and louder sing
> For every tatter in its mortal dress,

the metaphoric identification of an old man with a scarecrow jolts us out of all our usual unthinking attitudes about old men as kind, happy folk who are content to have passed from youth into age.

When we read "rose," we may more or less call to mind a picture of a rose, or perhaps we are reminded of the odor or texture of a rose. Whatever in a poem appeals to any of our senses (including sensations of heat and pressure as well as of sight, smell, taste, touch, sound) is an **image**. In short, images are the sensory content of a work, whether literal or figurative. When a poet says "My rose," and he is speaking about a rose, we have no figure of speech — though we still have an image. If, however, "My rose" is a shortened form of "My love is a rose," some would say that he is using a metaphor, but others would say that because the first term is omitted ("My love is"), the rose is a **symbol**. A poem about the transience of a rose might, for example, compel the reader to feel that the transience of female beauty is the larger theme even though it is never explicitly stated. This is John Ciardi's point when he speaks (p. 158) of "the poet's essential duplicity." "The poet," Ciardi explains, "pretends to be talking about one thing, and all the while he is talking about many others." The horse in "Stopping by Woods on a Snowy Evening" is a horse and is also, Ciardi suggests, "that order of life that does not understand why a man stops in the wintry middle of nowhere to watch the snow come down."

Some symbols are **conventional symbols**, people have agreed to accept them as standing for something other than their literal meanings: a poem about the cross would probably be about Christianity; similarly, the rose has long been a symbol for love. In Virginia Woolf's novel *Mrs. Dalloway*, the husband communicates his love by proffering this conventional symbol: "He was holding out flowers — roses, red and white roses. (But he could not bring himself to say he loved her; not in so many words.)" Objects that are not conventional symbols, however, may also give rise to rich, multiple, indefinable associations. The following poem uses the traditional symbol of the rose, but uses it in a nontraditional way.

WILLIAM BLAKE

The Sick Rose

O rose, thou art sick!
The invisible worm
That flies in the night,
In the howling storm,

Has found out thy bed   5
Of crimson joy,
And his dark secret love
Does thy life destroy.

One might perhaps argue that the worm is "invisible" (line 2) merely because it is hidden within the rose, but an "invisible worm / That flies in the night" is more than a long, slender, soft-bodied, creeping animal; and a rose that has, or is, a "bed / Of crimson joy" is more than a gardener's rose. Blake's worm and rose suggest things beyond themselves — a stranger, more vibrant world than the world we are usually aware of. One finds oneself half-thinking, for example, that the worm is male, the rose female, and the poem is about the violation of virginity. Or that the poem is about the destruction of beauty: woman's beauty, rooted in joy, is destroyed by a power that feeds on her. But these interpretations are not fully satisfying: the poem presents a worm and a rose, and yet it is not merely about a worm and a rose. These objects resonate, stimulating our thoughts toward something else, but the something else is elusive, whereas it is not elusive in Burns's "My love is like a red, red rose."

A symbol, then, is an image so loaded with significance that it is not simply literal, and it does not simply stand for something else; it is both itself *and* something else that it richly suggests, a kind of manifestation of something too complex or too elusive to be otherwise revealed. Blake's poem is about a blighted rose and at the same time about much more. In a symbol, as Thomas Carlyle wrote, "the Infinite is made to blend with the Finite, to stand visible, and as it were, attainable there."

Here is a student's essay on Blake's "The Sick Rose," relating the symbolism to the speaker and audience.

Speaker and Audience in "The Sick Rose"

Blake's "The Sick Rose" seems, on first reading, to be addressed to a rose, but despite "O rose" of the first line, further reading reveals two other audiences: the speaker, if he is not a madman, is addressing a special kind of rose, a rose that can listen, and, second, he is addressing himself. Another way of putting these points is to say that the rose is in some measure a woman, and second, it is in some measure any person, male or female, here including the speaker.

The first point, that the rose is no ordinary rose, is evident from the fact that it is attacked by an "invisible worm/ That flies in the night" and that feels a "dark secret love" for the rose. Of course the worm might be invisible merely because it is concealed within the rose, and the "bed" of line 5 might simply be a flower bed, but other words, such as "joy" (line 6) and "love" (line 7) serve to bring the rose and the worm close to the human world. The flower bed thus suggests a bed of love, or rather (since the love is specifically said to be "dark" and "secret" and destructive) a bed of lust. The worm suggests the destructive male, partly because it is

phallic, partly perhaps because the biblical tradition holds
that the serpent in the garden is male, and mostly because the
worm may reasonably be conceived of as different in sex from the
flower, the rose being conventionally female.

Thus far the poem would seem, then, to be addressed to a
woman, or at least to a rose that partakes of human female characteristics. But repeated rereading suggests that the poet is
not so much addressing something or someone in front of him, but
is thinking aloud. Despite "O rose," he is in good measure
addressing himself, meditating upon a fact of life. Beauty and
love are destroyed in the "night" and "howling storm" by furtive
lust ("dark secret love"). The first step beyond seeing the
rose and worm as merely a rose and a worm is to see them as also
a woman and a man; the next step is to see them as the beauty
that anyone, regardless of gender, may have, and the destruc-
tiveness that is similarly beyond gender. Because the speaker
is clearly so sympathetic to the object he addresses that he is
virtually soliloquizing, it is reasonable to say that the speaker
and his audience and his subject are one. He may reasonably be
thought of as thinking about a process that is going on inside
of himself, as well as about some external destruction of feminine
beauty by male lust.

The previous sentences, with their abstractions, may seem
far from the poem, and indeed their language and the language of
the poem are utterly different. But the language of the poem sets
up vibrations or emanations that may be legitimately pursued;
to say that the poem starts with a rose and a worm and leads us
back to the speaker and even to ourselves is scarcely an
exaggeration.

This essay on symbolism is temperate, but essays on symbolism often have a way of seeming far-fetched to instructors, just as, perhaps, instructors' classroom references to symbolism may at first seem far-fetched to students. As a rough rule of thumb, beware of saying X equals, or symbolizes, Y, unless there are rather evident and insistent connections between X and Y. One reference to the darkness of night does not justify your talking about the night as symbolic of evil; one reference to water does not justify your talking about water as symbolic of life-giving forces. But a pattern of contrasting references to day and night, or to water versus an arid landscape, calls for such interpretations. As John Ciardi points out (p. 162), Frost's *repetition* of "miles to go before I sleep" forces us to give the words more than their usual significance, transforms "miles" and "sleep" into symbols. Remember, too, that although some things by their nature are likely to be symbolic of certain qualities (e.g., railroad trains of unfeeling industrialism, stars of spiritual or intellectual illumination, water of life), we should not respond automatically to these things as we do to red and green traffic lights. The poet shapes our responses, and an automatic response may preclude a more appropriate response. For example, in Matthew Arnold's "To Marguerite — Continued," the sea plays an important role. The poem begins "Yes! in the sea of life enisled," and it ends with a reference to "The unplumbed, salt, estranging sea." In this poem Arnold conceives of men as islands, creatures tragically *separated* by water. The student who writes about the life-giving symbol of water in this poem ignores the fact that Arnold specifies that it estranges and is salty, that is, undrinkable. Such a reading will distort the poem more than will a reading that sees the water only as water rather than emblematic of the gulfs (figurative language keeps slipping in, even in analysis) that separate men. Mary McCarthy's comments on symbolism in fiction (pp. 60–61) are relevant here. Keep in mind the fact that in literature things *are*; they may also *represent*, but don't lose sight of what they are.

The arrangement of the parts, the manner of organization of the entire poem is its **structure.** Every poem has its own structure, but if we stand back from a given poem we may see that the structure is one of three common sorts: repetitive structure, narrative structure, or logical structure. **Repetitive structure** is especially common in lyrics that are sung, where a single state is repeated from stanza to stanza so that the stanzas are pretty much interchangeable. As we read through "Auld Lang Syne," for instance, we get reaffirmation rather than progression. Here is a passage from Whitman's *By Blue Ontario's Shore* that similarly has a repetitive structure:

> I will confront these shows of the day and night,
> I will know if I am to be less than they,
> I will see if I am not as majestic as they,
> I will see if I am not as subtle and real as they,
> I will see if I am to be less generous than they.

In a poem with a **narrative structure** (we are not talking about "narrative poems," poems that tell a story, such as *The Odyssey* or *The Rime of the Ancient Mariner*, but about a kind of lyric poem) there is a sense of advance. Blake's "The Sick Rose" (p. 108) is an example. What comes later in the poem could not come earlier. The poem seems to get somewhere, to settle down to an end. A lyric in which the speaker at first grieves and then derives some comfort from the thought that at least he was once in love similarly has a narrative structure. Here is a short but detailed examination by F. W. Bateson of a poem with narrative structure, Wordsworth's "A slumber did my spirit seal." Although "She" in line three is unnamed, it is customary to call her Lucy because that name is given in some other poems associated with this one in Wordsworth's *Lyrical Ballads*. The poem consists of two quatrains:

> A slumber did my spirit seal;
>   I had no human fears:
> She seemed a thing that could not feel
>   The touch of earthly years.
>
> No motion has she now, no force;
>   She neither hears nor sees;
> Rolled round in earth's diurnal course,
>   With rocks, and stones, and trees.

Bateson writes:

> The structural basis of the poem is clearly the contrast between the two verses. Verse one deals with the past (there are no less than four verbs in a past tense — *did, had, seemed, could*). Lucy had been such a vital person that the possibility of her growing old or dying

had not crossed Wordsworth's mind. Verse two concerns the present (in addition to the *now* in the first line there are three main verbs in the present tense — *has, hears, sees*). Lucy is dead. The invulnerable Ariel-like creature is now as lifeless and immobile as stocks and stones. And the contrast is emphasized by the repetition of *earth*: Lucy, who had seemed immune from the passage of *earthly years*, must now submit to *earth's diurnal course*. So far from escaping the *touch* of years she is now undergoing a daily contact with the earth. The use of the solemn Latinism *diurnal*, the only three-syllable word in this mainly monosyllabic poem, completes the contrast. But the final impression the poem leaves is not of two contrasting moods, but of a single mood mounting to a climax in the pantheistic magnificence of the last two lines. How then is the surface conflict reconciled? The metre certainly makes its contribution. The identity of the metrical pattern in the two verses — which is paralleled by the virtual identity of the word-order (1. 5 repeats 1. 1, abstract noun + verb + pronoun + abstract noun, 1. 6 repeats 1. 2, and 1. 8 and 1. 4 both have nouns but no verb) — suggests an underlying identity of mood. The gap between the two verses is also bridged by the negatives. There are no less than six negatives in the first six lines. Indeed, as the first line really means "I was not mentally awake," all the sentences are essentially negative propositions, until we reach the tremendous positive of the last two lines. Finally, the description of the living Lucy as a mere *thing* has prepared the transition to the dead Lucy who is passively *rolled*. The rhymes have no special significance, as far as I can see, but the alliterations should not be overlooked. The initial *s*'s in 1. 1. do not seem to me of much interest (it is much the weakest line in the poem), though they may be intentional, but the *r*'s in ll. 7–8 are masterly. There are no less than three initial *r*'s and four internal *r*'s in the last twelve words,* and they provide a kind of cohesive cement to the lines. The implication is that the pantheistic universe is solidly *one*. The parallel lines in verse one are without alliteration, and its absence confirms the suggestion of fragility in the living Lucy (a *thing* who can only be described in negative terms).

English Poetry (London, 1950), pp. 33–34

This essay comes from a chapter in which Mr. Bateson has been arguing for "the all-importance of meaning in poetry and the

---

* The *r*'s in *earth's diurnal course* are not sounded in modern English. Wordsworth, however, certainly sounded them. Hazlitt had found "a strong tincture of the northern *burr*" in his voice when they first met in 1798 (the year before "A slumber did my spirit seal" was written). See Hazlitt's "My First Acquaintance with Poets."

comparative insignificance of sound," hence perhaps his some-what driving, or no-nonsense, manner.

The third kind of structure commonly found is **logical structure.** The speaker argues a case, and he comes to some sort of conclusion. Probably the most famous example of a poem that moves to a resolution through an argument is Andrew Marvell's "To His Coy Mistress." The speaker begins, "Had we but world enough, and time" (i.e., "if"), and for twenty lines he sets forth what he might do. At the twenty-first line he says, "But," and he indicates that the preceding twenty lines, in the subjunctive, are not a description of a real condition. The real condition (as he sees it) is that Time oppresses us, and he sets this idea forth in lines 21–32. In line 34 he begins his conclusion, "Now there-fore," clinching it in line 45 with "Thus."

Here is another example of a poem with a logical structure.

JOHN DONNE

The Flea

Mark but this flea, and mark in this
How little that which thou deniest me is;
It sucked me first, and now sucks thee,
And in this flea our two bloods mingled be.
Thou knowest that this cannot be said   5
A sin, nor shame, nor loss of maidenhead;
 Yet this enjoys before it woo,
 And pampered swells with one blood made of two,
 And this, alas, is more than we would do.

O stay! Three lives in one flea spare,   10
Where we almost, yea, more than married are;
This flea is you and I, and this
Our marriage bed and marriage temple is.
Though parents grudge, and you, we're met
And cloistered in these living walls of jet.   15
 Though use make you apt to kill me,
 Let not to that, self-murder added be,
 And sacrilege, three sins in killing three.

Cruel and sudden! Hast thou since
Purpled thy nail in blood of innocence?   20

Wherein could this flea guilty be,
Except in that drop which it sucked from thee?
Yet thou triumph'st and saist that thou
Find'st not thyself, nor me, the weaker now.
   'Tis true. Then learn how false, fears be;   25
   Just so much honor, when thou yield'st to me,
   Will waste, as this flea's death took life from thee.

The speaker is a lover who begins by assuring his mistress that
sexual intercourse is of no more serious consequence than a flea
bite. Between the first and second stanzas the woman has appar-
ently threatened to kill the flea, moving the lover to exclaim in
line 10, "O stay! Three lives in one flea spare." In this second
stanza he reverses his argument, now insisting on the importance
of the flea, arguing that since it has bitten both man and woman
it holds some of their lives as well as its own. Unpersuaded of its
importance, the woman kills the flea between the second and
third stanzas; and the speaker uses her action to reinforce his
initial position, when he says, in line 25, the death of the flea
has no serious consequences, and her yielding to him will have
no worse consequences.

Among the commonest devices in poems with logical structure (although this device is employed elsewhere too) is **verbal
irony.** The speaker's words mean more or less the opposite of
what they seem to say. Sometimes it takes the form of **understatement** (as when Andrew Marvell's speaker remarks with
cautious wryness, "The grave's a fine and private place, / But
none, I think, do there embrace"), sometimes the form of **over-
statement,** or **hyperbole** (as when Donne's speaker says that in
the flea he and the lady are "more than married"). Another
common device in poems with a logical structure is **paradox:**
the assertion of an apparent contradiction, as in "This flea is you
and I." But again it must be emphasized that irony and paradox
are not limited to poems with a logical structure. In "Auld Lang
Syne," for instance, there is the paradox that the remembrance
of joy evokes a kind of sadness, and there is understatement in
"we've wandered mony a weary fitt," which stands (roughly) for
something much bigger, such as "we have had many painful
experiences." The student who wishes to see irony and paradox
examined as structural principles should consult Cleanth Brooks's
The Well-Wrought Urn.

CONCLUDING REMARKS
ON WRITING ABOUT POETRY

Writing about poetry may seem to be easier than writing about fiction or drama because most poems that the student encounters are fairly short. He can usually keep the entire work before his eyes, and he need not be endowed with an exceptional memory. But the brevity may be deceptive. Because most of us are not used to reading poetry, we overlook a good deal of the complexity. Prose (the point will be mentioned again) runs straight on, but poetry is always turning back on itself, complicating its pattern of sound and of meaning. Of course the prose of fiction is not the prose of a newspaper or of a history book; it too is not used merely as a vehicle to give information about something outside of itself; rather, as David Lodge indicates in his essay on *Hard Times*, word by word it builds its own world. (Another way of putting it: The words of newspapers and textbooks aim, or should aim, at being inconspicuous. They are a sort of window, or telescope, through which we see things, but generally we do not value them for themselves. We look beyond them. They are road signs, telling us where Boston is, or how to get to the expressway. But the words of a piece of literature, especially of a poem, are among the things we are looking at and looking for.) Still, fiction tells a story, and the story is a major part of its interest. One is not expected to dwell on each word in a story; the narrative line carries one forward. But in poetry one is supposed to delight in the words themselves or, better, in their combinations, as well as in the experience they point to. The poet assumes his readers will enjoy his virtuoso performance with words. Alexander Pope may not have been fully conscious of exactly what he was doing when he wrote "Die and endow a college or a cat," but he probably would have been delighted with F. W. Bateson's perceptive analysis (p. 99) of the line. (Quite likely Pope *was* fully conscious; the man who wrote the lines about Ajax and Camilla — see below, p. 119 — cared about the minutest problems of poetry. In any case, as Robert Frost has said, the poet deserves credit for anything good that is found in the poem.) A poet exploits more fully than does the writer of fiction such devices as alliteration and rhythm; a substantial part of the meaning of his work resides in them. Frost touched on this matter when he defined poetry as "what gets lost in translation." Auden touched on it when he said that his ideal reader notices misprints.

This is not to say that poetry is all sound and no sense but only that the sound plays a larger part in making the sense than it does in expository prose and even in fiction. The so-called musical qualities of poetry are among the hardest to discuss, for two reasons: firstly, we are not much aware of these resources because few of us write poetry, and we therefore sometimes do not notice them; secondly, when we do notice them, we are likely to talk wildly about them. Once we have learned that there is such a thing as onomatopoeia (see p. 124), we may too quickly find the sound echoing the sense, even when it does not. About the only advice one can give is this: Read the poem over and over, aloud at least a couple of times, and try to hear as well as see what is going on. But once you have noticed things, don't believe them until further rereading convinces you that they are really there. Be especially cautious about large claims for the effect of the sound of a single word. But keep a shrewd eye (and ear) open for the effects of combinations of sounds, such as those pointed out in Pope. Here is the first stanza of Walter Savage Landor's "Past Ruined Ilion" followed by some shrewd comments by Monroe Beardsley on the combinations of sounds.

> Past ruined Ilion Helen lives,
>   Alcestis rises from the shades;
> Verse calls them forth; 'tis verse that gives
>   Immortal youth to mortal maids.

Beardsley says:

> The "n" sound in "ruined Ilion Helen" ties them together in a single catastrophe. The "v" of "verse" and the "f" of "forth" bring them together, suggesting that the statement "Verse calls them forth" is naturally true. "Maids" is given irony because its meaning contrasts with the meaning of the two words that are connected with it, "shades" by rhyme and "mortal" by alliteration. The sound-parallelism of "Immortal" and "mortal" reinforces the slight paradox of the claim that the youth of the maid will outlive the maid.
>
> *Aesthetics* (New York, 1958), pp. 236–37

For example, notice that Beardsley says that "the 'n' sound in 'ruined Ilion Helen' ties them together in a single catastrophe." He does *not* say that the "n" sound is catastrophic or that it is mournful. He notes combinations, relationships between words, and he also relies on the meanings of the words. He can speak of "a single catastrophe" because "ruined" *means* ruined. Ilion is a vanished city, and Helen is long dead. He does not make extravagant claims for the inherent meaning of the "n" sound. But he has seen some connections, and he talks plausibly about them.

An explication or an anlysis of a single poem will normally require some comment on the sound patterns, but not every essay on poetry need concern itself with such patterns. Good papers can be written on the development of an image or of a motif in a group of poems, for example, Frost's use of woods or stars, or Yeats's use of the legend of Helen of Troy. A paper that traces a recurrent image or motif may reveal a meaning, generated by a group of poems, that is barely perceptible in a single poem. The essayist who takes on such a job is the sort of reader Yeats had in mind when he wrote in one of his prefaces, "I must leave my myths and images to explain themselves as the years go by and one poem lights up another." But whatever the topic and the approach, the essayist's goal is to illuminate.

RHYTHM AND VERSIFICATION:
A GLOSSARY OF TERMS

Rhythm (most simply, in English poetry, stresses at regular intervals) has a power of its own. A highly pronounced rhythm is common in such forms of poetry as charms, college yells, and lullabies; all of them are aimed at inducing a special effect magically. It is not surprising that *carmen*, the Latin word for verse or song, is also the Latin word for charm and the word from which "charm" is derived.

In much poetry rhythm is only half-heard, but its omnipresence is suggested by the fact that when poetry is printed it is customary to begin each line with a capital letter. Prose (from Latin *prorsus*, "forward," "straight on") keeps running across the paper until the right-hand margin is reached, and then, merely because the paper has given out, the writer or printer starts again at the left, with a small letter. But verse (Latin *versus*, "a turning") often ends well short of the right-hand margin, and the next line begins at the left — usually with a capital — not because paper has run out but because the rhythmic pattern begins again. Lines of poetry are continually reminding us that they have a pattern.

A word of caution: A mechanical, unvarying rhythm may be good to put the baby to sleep, but it can be deadly to readers who wish to keep awake. A poet varies his rhythm according to his purpose; he ought not to be so regular that he is (in W. H. Auden's words) an "accentual pest." In competent hands, rhythm contributes to meaning; it says something. Ezra Pound has a relevant comment: "Rhythm *must* have meaning. It can't be merely a careless dash off, with no grip and no real hold to the words and sense, a tumty tum tumty tum tum ta." Consider this description of Hell from *Paradise Lost* (stressed syllables are marked by /; unstressed syllables by ‿):

    Rocks, caves, lakes, fens, bogs, dens, and shades of death.

Milton immediately follows one heavy stress with another (in contrast to the iambic feet — alternating unstressed and stressed syllables — that are the norm in the poem), helping to communicate the "meaning" — the oppressive monotony of Hell. As a second example, consider the function of the rhythm in two lines by Alexander Pope:

    When Ajax strives some rock's vast weight to throw,

    The line too labors, and the words move slow.

The stressed syllables do not merely alternate with the unstressed ones; rather, the great weight of the rock is suggested by three consecutive stressed words, "rock's vast weight," and the great effort involved in moving it is suggested by another three consecutive stresses, "line too labors," and by yet another three, "words move slow." Note, also, the abundant pauses within the lines. In the first line, for example, unless one's speech is slovenly, one must pause at least slightly after "Ajax," "strives," "rock's," "vast," "weight," and "throw." The grating sounds in "Ajax" and "rock's" do their work, too, and so do the explosive *t*'s. When Pope wishes to suggest lightness, he reverses his procedure, and he groups *un*stressed syllables:

    Not so, when swift Camilla scours the plain,

    Flies o'er th' unbending corn, and skims along the main.

This last line has twelve syllables, and is thus longer than the line about Ajax, but the addition of "along" helps to communicate lightness and swiftness because in this line (it can be argued) neither of its syllables is strongly stressed. If "along" is omitted, the line still makes grammatical sense and becomes more "regular," but it also becomes less imitative of lightness.

The very regularity of a line may be meaningful too. Shakespeare begins a sonnet thus:

When I do count the clock that tells the time.

This line about a mechanism runs with appropriate regularity. (It is worth noting, too, that "count the clock" and "tells the time" emphasize the regularity by the repetition of sounds and syntax.) But notice what Shakespeare does in the middle of the next line:

And see the brave day sunk in hideous night.

The technical vocabulary of **prosody** (the study of the principles of verse structure, including meter, rhyme, and other sound effects, and stanzaic patterns) is large. An understanding of these terms will not turn anyone into a poet, but it will enable one to discuss some aspects of poetry more efficiently. The following are the chief terms of prosody.

Most English poetry has a pattern of **stressed** (accented) sounds, and this pattern is the **meter** (from the Greek word for "measure"). Although in Old English poetry (poetry written in England before the Norman-French Conquest in 1066) a line may have any number of unstressed syllables in addition to four stressed syllables, most poetry written in England since the Conquest not only has a fixed number of stresses in a line but also a fixed number of unstressed syllables before or after each stressed one. (One really ought not to talk of "unstressed" or "unaccented" syllables, since to utter a syllable — however lightly — is to give it some stress. But the fact is that "unstressed" or "unaccented" are parts of the established terminology of versification.)

In a line of poetry the **foot** is the basic unit of measurement. It is on rare occasions a single stressed syllable; but generally a foot consists of two or three syllables, one of which is stressed. The repetition of feet, then, produces a pattern of stresses throughout the poem.

Two Cautions:

1. A poem will seldom contain only one kind of foot throughout; significant variations usually occur, but one kind of foot is dominant.

2. In reading a poem, one pays attention to the sense as well as to the metrical pattern. By paying attention to the sense, one often finds that the stress falls on a word that according to the metrical pattern would be unstressed. Or a word that according to the pattern would be stressed may be seen to be unstressed. Furthermore, by reading for sense one finds that not all stresses are equally heavy; some are almost as light as unstressed syllables, and sometimes there is a **hovering stress,** that is, the stress is equally distributed over two adjacent syllables. To repeat: One reads for sense, allowing the syntax to help indicate the stresses.

The most common feet in English poetry are:

iamb (adjective: **iambic**): one unstressed syllable followed by one stressed syllable. The iamb, said to be the most common pattern in English speech, is surely the most common in English poetry. It is called a **rising meter,** the foot rising toward the stress. The following example has five iambic feet:

I saw | the sky | descend | ing black | and white. (Robert Lowell)

trochee (**trochaic**): one stressed syllable followed by one un-stressed; a **falling meter,** the foot falling away from the stress.

Let her | live to | earn her | dinners.   (J. M. Synge)

anapest (**anapestic**): two unstressed syllables followed by one stressed; a rising meter.

There are man | y who say | that a dog | has his day.
(Dylan Thomas)

dactyl (**dactylic**): one stressed syllable followed by two un-stressed; a falling meter. This tri-syllabic foot, like the anapest, is common in light verse or verse suggesting joy, but its use is not limited to such material. Thomas Hood's sentimental "The Bridge of Sighs" begins:

Take her up | tenderly.   (Hood)

spondee (**spondaic**): two stressed syllables; most often used as a substitute for an iamb or trochee; it neither rises nor falls.

Smart lad, | to slip | betimes | away.   (A. E. Housman)

Because the **pyrrhic** foot (two unstressed syllables) lacks a stress, it is often not considered a legitimate foot in English.

A metrical line consists of one or more feet and is named for the number of feet in it. The following names are used:

monometer:	one foot	**pentameter:**	five feet
dimeter:	two feet	**hexameter:**	six feet
trimeter:	three feet	**heptameter:**	seven feet
tetrameter:	four feet	**octameter:**	eight feet

A line is scanned for the kind and number of feet in it, and the **scansion** tells you if it is, say, anapestic trimeter (three anapests):

$$\breve{\text{As}} \ \breve{\text{I}} \ \acute{\text{came}} \mid \breve{\text{to}} \ \breve{\text{the}} \ \acute{\text{edge}} \mid \breve{\text{of}} \ \breve{\text{the}} \ \acute{\text{woods.}} \quad \text{(Frost)}$$

Another example, this time iambic pentameter:

$$\breve{\text{Since}} \ \acute{\text{brass,}} \ \breve{\text{nor}} \ \acute{\text{stone,}} \ \breve{\text{nor}} \ \acute{\text{earth,}} \ \breve{\text{nor}} \ \acute{\text{boundless}} \ \breve{}\ \acute{\text{sea.}} \ \text{(Shakespeare)}$$

A line ending with a stress has a **masculine ending;** a line ending with an extra unstressed syllable has a **feminine ending.** The lines above by Synge and Hood have feminine endings; those by Lowell, Thomas, Housman, Frost, and Shakespeare have masculine endings. The **caesura** (usually indicated by the symbol //) is a slight pause within the line. It need not be indicated by punctuation, and it does not affect the metrical count:

> Awake, my St. John! // leave all meaner things
> To low ambition, // and the pride of kings.
> Let us // (since Life can little more supply
> Than just to look about us // and to die)
> Expatiate free // o'er all this scene of Man;
> A mighty maze! // but not without a plan;
> A wild, // where weeds and flowers promiscuous shoot;
> Or garden, // tempting with forbidden fruit.   (Pope)

The varying position of the caesura helps to give Pope's lines an informality that plays against the formality of the pairs of rhyming lines.

An **end-stopped line** concludes with a distinct syntactical pause, but a **run-on line** has its sense carried over into the next line without syntactical pause. (The running-on of a line is called **enjambment.**) In the following passage, only the first is a run-on line:

> Yet if we look more closely we shall find
> Most have the seeds of judgment in their mind:
> Nature affords at least a glimmering light;
> The lines, though touched but faintly, are drawn right.　　(Pope)

Meter produces **rhythm,** recurrences at equal intervals, but rhythm (from a Greek word meaning "flow") is usually applied to larger units than feet. Often it depends most obviously on pauses. Thus, a poem with run-on lines will have a different rhythm from a poem with end-stopped lines, even though both are in the same meter. And prose, though it is unmetrical, can thus have rhythm, too. In addition to being affected by syntactical pause, rhythm is affected by pauses due to consonant clusters and the length of words. Polysyllabic words establish a different rhythm from monosyllabic words, even in metrically identical lines. One can say, then, that rhythm is altered by shifts in meter, syntax, and the length and ease of pronunciation. But even with no such shift, even if a line is repeated verbatim, a reader may sense a change in rhythm. The rhythm of the final line of a poem, for example, may well differ from that of the line before, even though in all other respects the lines are identical, as in Frost's "Stopping by Woods on a Snowy Evening," which concludes by repeating "And miles to go before I sleep." One may simply sense that this final line ought to be spoken, say, more slowly.

Though rhythm is basic to poetry, **rhyme** is not. Rhyme is the repetition of the identical or similar stressed sound or sounds. It is, presumably, pleasant in itself; it suggests order; and it also may be related to meaning, for it brings two words sharply together, often implying a relationship, like, for example, Pope's "throne" and "alone." **Perfect** or **exact rhymes** occur when differing consonant-sounds are followed by identical stressed vowel-sounds, and the following sounds, if any, are identical (foe: toe; meet: fleet; buffer: rougher). Note that perfect rhyme involves identity of sound, not of spelling. "Fix" and "sticks," like "buffer" and "rougher," are perfect rhymes.

Half-rhyme (or **slant-rhyme, approximate-rhyme, near-rhyme, off-rhyme**): only the final consonant-sounds of the rhyming words are identical; the stressed vowel-sounds as well as the initial consonant-sounds, if any, differ (soul: oil; mirth: forth; trolley: bully). **Eye-rhyme** is not really rhyme; it merely looks like rhyme (cough: bough: rough). **Masculine rhyme:** the final syllables are stressed and, after their differing initial consonant-sounds, are identical in sound (stark: mark; support: retort). **Feminine rhyme** (or **double-rhyme**): stressed rhyming syllables are followed by identical unstressed syllables (revival: arrival; flatter: batter). **Triple-rhyme:** a kind of feminine rhyme in which identical stressed vowel-sounds are followed by two identical unstressed syllables (machinery: scenery; tenderly: slenderly). **End-rhyme** (or **terminal-rhyme**) has the rhyming word at the end of the line. **Internal rhyme** has at least one of the rhyming words within the line (Wilde's "Each narrow *cell* in which we *dwell*"). **Alliteration** is sometimes defined as the repetition of initial sounds ("All the *aw*ful *au*guaries" or "*B*ring me my *b*ow of *b*urning gold"), sometimes as the prominent repetition of a consonant ("a*f*ter li*f*e's *f*it*f*ul *f*ever"). **Assonance:** identical vowel-sounds preceded and followed by differing consonant-sounds, in words in proximity. Whereas "tide" and "hide" are rhymes, "tide" and "mine" are assonantal. **Consonance:** identical consonant-sounds and differing vowel-sounds in words in proximity (fail: feel; rough: roof; pitter: patter). Sometimes consonance is more loosely defined merely as the repetition of a consonant (fai*l*: pee*l*). **Onomatopoeia** is said to occur when the sound of a word echoes or suggests the meaning of a word. "Hiss" and "buzz" are onomatopoetic. There is a mistaken tendency to see onomatopoeia everywhere, for example, in "thunder" and "horror." Many words sometimes thought to be onomatopoetic are not clearly imitative of the thing they denote; they merely contain some sounds which — when we know what the word means — seem to have some resemblance to the thing they denote. Tennyson's lines from "Come down, O maid" are usually cited as an example of onomatopoeia:

> The moan of doves in immemorial elms
> And murmuring of innumerable bees.

But John Crowe Ransom has pointed out that if many of the sounds of "murmuring of innumerable bees" are reproduced in a line of different meaning — "murdering of innumerable beeves" — the suggestiveness is lost.

Lines of poetry are commonly arranged in a rhythmical unit called a **stanza** (from an Italian word meaning a "room" or "stopping-place"). Usually all the stanzas in a poem have the same rhyme pattern. A stanza is sometimes called a **verse**, though "verse" may also mean a single line of poetry. (In discussing stanzas, rhymes are indicated by identical letters. Thus, *abab* indicates that the first and third lines rhyme with each other, while the second and fourth lines are linked by a different rhyme. *x* is used to denote an unrhymed line.) Common stanzaic forms in English poetry are the following:

couplet: stanza of two lines, usually, but not necessarily with end-rhymes. "Couplet" is also used for a pair of rhyming lines. The **octosyllabic couplet** is iambic or trochaic tetrameter:

Had we but world enough, and time,
This coyness, lady, were no crime.   (Marvell)

heroic couplet: a rhyming couplet of iambic pentameter, often "closed," that is, containing a complete thought, there being a fairly heavy pause at the end of the first line and a still heavier one at the end of the second. Commonly, there is a parallel or an antithesis within a line, or between the two lines. It is called heroic because in England, especially in the eighteenth century, it was much used for heroic (epic) poems.

Some foreign writers, some our own despise;
The ancient only, or the moderns, prize.   (Pope)

triplet (or **tercet**): a three-line stanza, usually with one rhyme.

Whenas in silks my Julia goes
Then, then (methinks) how sweetly flows
That liquefaction of her clothes.   (Herrick)

quatrain: a four-line stanza, rhymed or unrhymed. The **heroic** (or **elegiac**) **quatrain** is iambic pentameter, rhyming *abab*. The **ballad stanza** is a quatrain alternating iambic tetrameter with iambic trimeter lines, usually rhyming *abxb*. Sometimes it is followed by a **refrain**, a line or lines repeated several times.

sonnet: a fourteen-line poem, predominantly in iambic pentameter. The rhyme is usually according to one of the two following schemes. The **Italian** (or **Petrarchan**) **sonnet** has two divisions: the first eight lines (rhyming *abba abba*) are the **octave**, the last six (rhyming *cd cd cd*, or a variant) are the **sestet**. Keats's "On First Looking into Chapman's Homer" (p. 104) is an Italian sonnet. The second kind of sonnet, the **English** (or **Shakespearean**) **sonnet**, is usually arranged into three quatrains and a couplet, rhyming *abab cdcd efef gg*. In many sonnets there is a marked correspondence between the rhyme scheme and the development of the thought. Thus an Italian sonnet may state a generalization in the octave and a specific example in the sestet. Or an English sonnet may give three examples — one in each quatrain — and draw a conclusion in the couplet.

A good deal of English poetry is unrhymed, much of it in **blank verse,** that is, unrhymed iambic pentameter. Introduced into English poetry by Surrey in the middle of the sixteenth century, late in the century it became the standard medium (especially in the hands of Marlowe and Shakespeare) of English drama. In the seventeenth century, Milton used it for *Paradise Lost,* and it has continued to be used in both dramatic and nondramatic literature. For an example see the passage from Milton on p. 100. A passage of blank verse that has a rhetorical unity is sometimes called a **verse paragraph.**

The second kind of unrhymed poetry fairly common in English, especially in the twentieth century, is **free verse** (or *vers libre*): rhythmical lines varying in length, adhering to no fixed metrical pattern and usually unrhymed. The pattern is often largely based on repetition and parallel grammatical structure. Though such a form may appear unrestrained, as T. S. Eliot (a practitioner) has said, "No *vers* is *libre* for the man who wants to do a good job." For a sample of free verse, see the passage from Whitman on p. 112.

PART THREE

6

SAMPLE ESSAYS

The six essays given below are not offered as models of superb writing. They are offered as examples of the sort of writing that students may be expected to do. But in two matters the students must better four of them: because the selections by Lodge, Daiches, Rosen, and Krutch have been extracted from larger studies, they do not have the neat opening and closing paragraphs that a good independent essay has. (Ciardi's discussion is complete — as is Van Doren's, except that in its references to other poets Van Doren's glances back to some earlier essays in his book.)

The two essays on fiction reveal different approaches. David Lodge, using the textural approach, looks at a page from Dickens' *Hard Times*, giving it the sort of close reading that is commonly reserved for poetry. He shows how Dickens makes every word contribute to his portrait of Gradgrind and how the portrait contributes to the novel's central concern. David Daiches, using the structural approach, stands a little further back from his subject, surveying an entire story by following the development of its theme. Where Lodge looks hard at the words, Daiches looks hard at the episodes. (Lodge, of course, has ideas about the theme of the novel as a whole, and Daiches has ideas about the words or he could not detect a theme, but the treatments are different.)

The two essays on drama also differ in overall approach. William Rosen examines Shakespeare's characterization of King

Lear in the first scene, more or less as a spectator in the theater
might perceive it. Rosen's interpretation is doubtless conditioned
by what he knows of the entire play, but he confines himself to a
single scene, and he does not attempt in these pages to discuss
the larger topics of "The Character of King Lear" and "Tech-
niques of Characterization in *King Lear*." He does one thing at
a time. Joseph Wood Krutch ranges over Arthur Miller's *Death
of a Salesman* and Tennessee Williams' *A Streetcar Named
Desire*, seeking to get at the broad underlying ideas and to place
them in a tradition of tragic drama.

Each of the two essays on poetry looks closely at a short poem.
Mark Van Doren, after an awkward start ("is *not . . . not . . .
un- . . . .* Perha*p*s no *p*oem is *p*erfect . . . *p*erha*p*s . . . a*pp*earance
. . . *p*erfection . . . sus*p*icious a*pp*earance . . . *p*oem . . . *p*ut" —
all this within two sentences), seeks to demonstrate that "the
poem as a whole is fine, but . . . [it] goes steadily downhill."
After an initial paragraph on the origin of the poem and a second
paragraph on the motif of solitude, he moves forward stanza by
stanza. (The comparison with Pound, Whitman, and Peele in
the second paragraph may seem arbitrary and undeveloped, but
Mr. Van Doren had earlier in his book discussed some of their
poems.) Part of the excellence of this essay is in the judicious
balancing of praise and blame. It is easy to write an attack but
hard to keep the reader from wondering why you are bothering
to write about something you dislike, and it is hard to avoid
sounding supercilious. Mr. Van Doren, even while commenting
adversely, keeps us aware of his respect for the work; he never
allows us to think that he believes he is superior to the thing he
is discussing. Mr. Ciardi, with a vigor and a breeziness that come
from having established himself as a poet and a critic, examines
Robert Frost's "Stopping by Woods on a Snowy Evening." Mr.
Ciardi's essay, as he points out at the start, is about poetry; and
his remarks about Frost's poem are offered in the course of
making the point that poetry is "duplicity." Reasonably, then,
after he finishes his discussion of "Stopping by Woods," he
returns, in his last paragraph, to some discussion of "every truly
good poem."

Finally, it should be mentioned that there is no reason to
believe that any of these six authors came by his ideas easily or
quickly. Let the student take encouragement from Einstein's
answer to a question: "How do I work? I grope." And from
Robert Frost: "Education is turning things over in the mind."

DAVID LODGE

The Rhetoric of a Page of Hard Times

The very first chapter of *Hard Times* affords an excellent illustration of Dickens's rhetoric, and it is short enough to be quoted and analysed in its entirety.

HARD TIMES

BOOK THE FIRST. SOWING
CHAPTER I
THE ONE THING NEEDFUL

'Now, what I want is, Facts. Teach these boys and girls nothing but Facts. Facts alone are wanted in life. Plant nothing else, and root out everything else. You can only form the minds of reasoning animals upon Facts: nothing else will ever be of any service to them. This is the principle on which I bring up my own children, and this is the principle on which I bring up these children. Stick to Facts, Sir!'

The scene was a plain, bare, monotonous vault of a schoolroom, and the speaker's square forefinger emphasised his observations by underscoring every sentence with a line on the schoolmaster's sleeve. The emphasis was helped by the speaker's square wall of a forehead, which had his eyebrows for its base, while his eyes found commodious cellarage in two dark caves, overshadowed by the wall. The emphasis was helped by the speaker's mouth, which was wide, thin, and hard set. The emphasis was helped by the speaker's voice, which was inflexible, dry, and dictatorial. The emphasis was helped by the speaker's hair, which bristled on the skirts of his bald head, a plantation of firs to keep the wind from its shining surface, all covered with knobs, like the crust of a plum pie, as if the head had scarcely warehouseroom for the hard facts stored inside. The speaker's obstinate carriage, square coat, square legs, square shoulders — nay, his very neckcloth, trained to take him by the throat with an unaccommodating grasp, like a stubborn fact, as it was — all helped the emphasis.

'In this life, we want nothing but Facts, Sir; nothing but Facts!'

The speaker, and the schoolmaster, and the third grown person present, all backed a little, and swept with their eyes the inclined plane of little vessels then and there arranged in order, ready to have imperial gallons of facts poured into them until they were full to the brim.

Reprinted from *Language of Fiction* (pp. 148–152) by David Lodge by permission of Columbia University Press and Routledge & Kegan Paul Ltd. Copyright 1966, Columbia University Press. (The title of this essay is the editor's.)

This chapter communicates, in a remarkably compact way, both a description and a judgment of a concept of education. This concept is defined in a speech, and then evaluated — not in its own terms, but in terms of the speaker's appearance and the setting. Dickens, of course, always relies heavily on the popular, perhaps primitive, assumption that there is a correspondence between a person's appearance and his character; and as Gradgrind is a governor of the school, its design may legitimately function as a metaphor for his character. Dickens also had a fondness for fancifully appropriate names, but — perhaps in order to stress the representativeness of Gradgrind's views — he does not reveal the name in this first chapter.[1]

Because of the brevity of the chapter, we are all the more susceptible to the effect of its highly rhetorical patterning, particularly the manipulation of certain repeated words, notably *fact*, *square*, and *emphasis*. The kind of education depicted here is chiefly characterized by an obsession with facts. The word occurs five times in the opening speech of the first paragraph, and it is twice repeated towards the end of the second, descriptive paragraph to prepare for the reintroduction of Gradgrind speaking — ' "we want nothing but Facts, Sir; nothing but Facts" '; and it occurs for the tenth and last time towards the end of the last paragraph. In Gradgrind's speeches the word is capitalized, to signify his almost religious devotion to Facts.

Gradgrind's concept of education is further characterized in ways we can group into three categories, though of course they are closely connected:

(1) It is authoritarian, fanatical and bullying in its application.
(2) It is rigid, abstract and barren in quality.
(3) It is materialistic and commercial in its orientation.

The first category is conveyed by the structure of the second paragraph, which is dominated by 'emphasis'. This paragraph comprises six sentences. In the first sentence we are told how the 'speaker's square forefinger emphasised his observations'. The

---

[1] Mary McCarthy has suggested that an anonymous 'he' at the beginning of a novel usually moves the reader to sympathetic identification. That the effect is quite the reverse in this example shows that the effect of any narrative strategy is determined finally by the narrator's language.

next four, central sentences are each introduced, with cumulative force, by the clause 'The emphasis was helped', and this formula, translated from the passive to the active voice, makes a fittingly 'emphatic' conclusion to the paragraph in the sixth sentence: 'all helped the emphasis'. This rhetorical pattern has a dual function. In one way it reflects or imitates Gradgrind's own bullying, over-emphatic rhetoric, of which we have an example in the first para-graph; but in another way it helps to *condemn* Gradgrind, since it 'emphasises' the narrator's own pejorative catalogue of details of the speaker's person and immediate environment. The narra-tor's rhetoric is, as it must be, far more skilful and persuasive than Gradgrind's.

The qualities in category (2) are conveyed in a number of geometrical or quasi-geometrical terms, *wide, line, thin, base, surface, inclined plane* and, particularly, *square* which recurs five times; and in words suggestive of barren regularity, *plain, bare, monotonous, arranged in order, inflexible.* Such words are par-ticularly forceful when applied to human beings — whether Gradgrind or the children. The metamorphosis of the human into the non-human is, as we shall find confirmed later, one of Dickens's main devices for conveying his alarm at the way Victorian society was moving.

Category (3), the orientation towards the world of com-merce, is perhaps less obvious than the other categories, but it is unmistakably present in some of the boldest tropes of the chapter: *commodious cellarage, warehouse room, plantation, ves-sels, imperial gallons.*

The authoritarian ring of '*imperial*' leads us back from cate-gory (3) to category (1), just as '*under-scoring* every sentence with a *line*' leads us from (1) to (2). There is a web of connect-ing strands between the qualities I have tried to categorize: it is part of the rhetorical strategy of the chapter that all the qualities it evokes are equally applicable to Gradgrind's character, person, ideas, his school and the children (in so far as he has shaped them in his own image).

Metaphors of growth and cultivation are of course common-place in discussion of education, and we should not overlook the ironic invocation of such metaphors, with a deliberately religious, prophetic implication (reinforced by the Biblical echo of the chapter heading, 'The One Thing Needful'[2]) in the title of the

[2] Chapter ii of Book I is called "Murdering the Innocents."

Book, 'SOWING', later to be followed by Book the Second, 'REAPING', and Book the Third, 'GARNERING'. These metaphors are given a further twist in Gradgrind's recommendation to 'Plant nothing else and root out everything else' (except facts).

If there is a flaw in this chapter it is the simile of the plum pie, which has pleasant, genial associations alien to the character of Gradgrind, to whose head it is, quite superfluously, applied. Taken as a whole, however, this is a remarkably effective and densely woven beginning of the novel.

The technique of the first chapter of *Hard Times* could not be described as 'subtle'. But subtle effects are often lost in a first chapter, where the reader is coping with the problem of 'learning the author's language'. Perhaps with some awareness of this fact, sharpened by his sense of addressing a vast, popular audience, Dickens begins many of his novels by nailing the reader's attention with a display of sheer rhetorical power, relying particularly on elaborate repetition. One thinks, for instance, of the fog at the beginning of *Bleak House* or the sun and shadow in the first chapter of *Little Dorrit*. In these novels the rhetoric works to establish a symbolic atmosphere; in *Hard Times*, to establish a thematic Idea — the despotism of Fact. But this abstraction — Fact — is invested with a remarkable solidity through the figurative dimension of the language.

The gross effect of the chapter is simply stated, but analysis reveals that it is achieved by means of a complex verbal activity that is far from simple. Whether it represents fairly any actual educational theory or practice in mid-nineteenth-century England is really beside the point. It aims to convince us of the *possibility* of children being taught in such a way, and to make us recoil from the imagined possibility. The chapter succeeds or fails as rhetoric; and I think it succeeds.

Dickens begins as he means to continue. Later in the novel we find Gradgrind's house, which, like the school-room, is a function of himself, described in precisely the same terms of fact and rigid measurement, partly geometrical and partly commercial.

> A very regular feature on the face of the country, Stone Lodge was. Not the least disguise toned down or shaded off that uncompromising fact in the landscape. A great square house, with a heavy portico darkening the principal windows, as its master's heavy brows over-shadowed his eyes. A calculated, cast up, balanced and proved house. Six windows on this side of the door, six on that side; a total of twelve in this wing, a total of twelve in the other wing; four and

twenty carried over to the back wings. A lawn and garden and an
infant avenue, all ruled straight like a botanical account-book.
(I, iii)

It has been observed that Dickens individualizes his characters
by making them use peculiar locutions and constructions in their
speech, a technique which was particularly appropriate to serial
publication in which the reader's memory required to be frequently jogged. This technique extends beyond the idiosyncratic
speech of characters, to the language in which they are described.
A key-word, or group of key-words, is insistently used when the
character is first introduced, not only to identify him but also to
evaluate him, and is invoked at various strategic points in the subsequent action. Dickens's remarkable metaphorical inventiveness
ensures that continuity and rhetorical emphasis are not obtained
at the expense of monotony. The application of the key-words
of the first chapter to Mr. Gradgrind's house gives the same
delight as the development of a metaphysical conceit. The observation that Mrs. Gradgrind, 'whenever she showed a symptom
of coming to life, was invariably stunned by some weighty piece
of fact tumbling on her' (I, iv), affords a kind of verbal equivalent of knock-about comedy, based on a combination of expec-
tancy (we know the word will recur) and surprise (we are not
prepared for the particular formulation).

DAVID DAICHES

The Theme of "The Dead"

In "The Dead" Joyce uses a much more expansive technique
than he does elsewhere in *Dubliners*. He is not here merely concerned with shaping a series of events into a unity; he has a
specific point to make — a preconceived theme in terms of which
the events in "The Dead" are selected and arranged. In the other
stories there is no point other than the pattern that emerges from
his telling of the story; no argument can be isolated and discussed
as the "theme" of the story, for the story is the theme and the
theme is the story. The insight of the artist organizes the data
provided by observation into a totality, but no external principle

Reprinted from *The Novel and the Modern World*, Revised Edition
(1960), by David Daiches, by permission of The University of Chicago
Press. Copyright 1960 The University of Chicago Press. (The title of
this essay is the editor's.)

determines that organization; the principle of organization is determined simply by further contemplation of the data themselves. But "The Dead" is the working-out, in terms of realistic narrative, of a preconceived theme, and that theme is a man's withdrawal into the circle of his own egotism, a number of external factors trying progressively to break down the walls of that circle, and those walls being finally broken down by the culminating assault on his egotism coming simultaneously from without, as an incident affecting him, and from within, as an increase of understanding. Only when we have appreciated this theme does the organization of the story become intelligible to us. On the surface it is the story of Gabriel returning from a jolly time at a party given by his aunts in a mood of desire for his wife and the frustration of that desire on his learning that a song sung by one of the guests at the party had reminded his wife of a youth who had been in love with her many years ago and who had died of pneumonia caught through standing outside her window in the cold and the rain; so that his wife is thinking of that past, in which Gabriel had no share, when he was expecting her to be giving herself to him, the final result being that Gabriel loses his mood of desire and falls asleep in a mood of almost impersonal understanding. But about three-quarters of the story is taken up with a vivid and detailed account of the party, and on first reading the story we are puzzled to know why Joyce devotes so much care and space to the party if the ending is to be simply Gabriel's change of mood on learning how his wife is really feeling. As a piece of simple patterning the story seems lopsided; we have to discover the central theme before we realize how perfectly proportioned the story is.

The theme of the story is the assault on the walled circle of Gabriel's egotism. The first character we see is Lily, the caretaker's daughter, rushed almost off her feet in the performance of her various duties. Then comes a pause, and Joyce turns to describe the Misses Morkan, who are giving the party, and the nature of the function. Then, when this retrospect had been brought up to the time of the opening of the story, Gabriel and his wife enter — late for the party, everyone expecting them. The external environment is drawn first before Gabriel enters and makes it merely an environment for himself. Lily is an independent personality, quite outside Gabriel's environment; she is introduced before Gabriel in order that when Gabriel arrives the

reader should be able to feel the contrast between the environment as Gabriel feels it to be (a purely personal one), and as it
is to a quite objective observer — the caretaker's daughter to
whom the party is just an increase of work. Gabriel is greeted as
he enters with a great deal of fuss; he enters naturally into the
environment his aunts are preparing for him, but immediately
after the greeting he has an illuminating encounter with Lily.
He patronizes her, as he had known her since she was a child.
He remarks gaily that one of these days he will be going to her
wedding. Lily resents the remark and replies bitterly that "the
men that is now is only all palaver and what they can get out of
you."

What part does this little incident play in the story? It is the
first attempt to break down the circle of Gabriel's egotism. He
has questioned Lily, not with any sincere desire to learn about
her, but in order to indulge his own expansive mood. He does not
recognize that Lily and her world exist in their own right; to him
they are merely themes for his genial conversation. Gabriel colors
at Lily's reply; his egotism is hurt ever so slightly, but the fortress
is still very far from taken. How slight the breach was is illustrated by his subsequent action — he thrusts a coin into the girl's
hand, warming himself in the glow of his own generosity and
not concerned with finding a method of giving that will obviate
any embarrassment on Lily's part. On thinking over his encounter
with Lily he sees it simply as a failure on his part to take up the
right tone, and this failure of his own hurts his pride a little and
makes him wonder whether he ought not to change the speech
he has prepared for after dinner — perhaps that is the wrong
tone too. He sees the whole incident from a purely egotistical
point of view; Lily exists only as an excuse for his gesturing, and
he is worried lest his gestures are not those which will get most
appreciation from his audience.

Then we have Gabriel again in his relation with his aunts.
He was always their favorite nephew, we are told. We see his
possessive attitude to Gretta, his wife. We see him patting his tie
reassuringly when his wife shows a tendency to laugh at him.
When that tendency is manifested by Aunt Julia as well he shows
signs of anger, and tactful Aunt Kate changes the conversation.
The picture of Gabriel as withdrawn behind the walls of his own
egotism is carefully built up.

The second assault on Gabriel's egotism is made by Miss

Ivors, the Irish Nationalist, who attacks his individualism and asks what he is doing for his people and his country. She succeeds in making Gabriel very uncomfortable, and when she leaves him he tries to banish all thought of the conversation from his memory with the reflection that "of course the girl, or woman, or whatever she was, was an enthusiast but there was a time for all things." He goes on to reflect that "she had tried to make him ridiculous before people, heckling him and staring at him with her rabbit's eyes." And so fails the second attempt to break down the circle of Gabriel's egotism.

Then we see Gabriel in a more congenial atmosphere, where his egotism is safe. He is asked to carve the goose — as usual. But Gabriel has been upset, and his cold refusal of a request by Gretta shows his egotism on the defensive. He runs over the heads of his speech in his mind. It must be changed — changed in such a way as to squash these assaults that are being made on his ego. And so he thinks up a nice, cozy talk about hospitality and humor and humanity and the virtues of the older generation (with which, as against the generation represented by Miss Ivors, he temporarily identifies himself). Eventually the meal begins, and Gabriel takes his seat at the head of the table, thoroughly at ease at last.

Mr. Bartell D'Arcy is Gabriel's counterpart — a figure merely sketched, to serve the part of a symbol in the story. There is deliberate irony on Joyce's part in making Gretta refer to him as conceited in an early conversation with Gabriel. When at dinner a group of guests are discussing with their hostesses the singers of Ireland, their complacency is such as to dismiss Caruso almost with contempt: they had hardly heard of him. Only D'Arcy suggests that Caruso might be better than any of the singers mentioned, and his suggestion is met with skepticism. D'Arcy alone of the guests refuses to drink either port or sherry until persuaded by nudges and whispers. And it is D'Arcy who sings the song that removes Gretta to another world.

Gabriel's speech takes place as planned, and for some time he revels happily in the little world of which he is the center. The party ends and the guests stand with coats on in the hall, about to take their leave. Gabriel is waiting for Gretta to get ready, and as he and others are waiting the sound of someone playing the piano comes down to the hall:

"Who's playing up there?" asked Gabriel.

"Nobody. They're all gone."

"O no, Aunt Kate," said Mary Jane. "Bartell D'Arcy and Miss O'Callaghan aren't gone yet."

"Someone is fooling at the piano anyhow," said Gabriel.

D'Arcy is first "nobody"; then — and it is significant for the structure of the story that it is Gabriel who says this — he is "fooling at the piano." While Gabriel, a little disturbed again, is making a final effort to re-establish his full sense of his own importance by telling a humorous story to the circle in the hall and thus becoming again the center of attraction, the sound of someone singing comes downstairs, and Gabriel sees his wife listening, standing near the top of the first flight "as if she were a symbol of something." D'Arcy stops abruptly on being discovered (again the contrast with Gabriel) and finally Gabriel and Gretta set out for the hotel where they are to spend the night, as it is too far to go home at such an hour.

Then comes the climax, when the fortified circle of Gabriel's egotism is battered down by a series of sharp blows. Just at the moment of his greatest self-confidence and desire for her, Gretta tells him that she is thinking about the song D'Arcy had sung. He questions her, first genially, and then, as he begins to realize the implications of the song for Gretta, more and more coldly:

"I am thinking about a person long ago who used to sing that song."

"And who was the person long ago?" asked Gabriel, smiling.

"It was a person I used to know in Galway when I was living with my grandmother," she said.

The smile passed away from Gabriel's face. . . .

Miss Ivor has talked about Galway; it was one of the symbols of that world of otherness against which Gabriel had been shutting himself in all evening. This is the beginning of the final assault. Then Gabriel learns that the "person" was a young boy that Gretta used to know, long before she knew him. He had been in love with her, and they used to go out walking together. With cold irony Gabriel asks whether that was the reason that Gretta had earlier in the evening expressed a desire to go to Galway for the summer holidays. When she tells him that the young man is dead — dying long since, when he was only seventeen — this line of defense is taken away from Gabriel and he falls back onto his final line:

> "What was he?" asked Gabriel, still ironically.
> "He was in the gasworks," she said.
> Gabriel felt humiliated by the failure of his irony and by the evocation of this figure from the dead, a boy in the gasworks.

Gabriel has no further defenses left. He burns with shame, seeing himself

> as a ludicrous figure, acting as a pennyboy for his aunts, a nervous, well-meaning sentimentalist, orating to vulgarians and idealising his own clownish lusts, the pitiable fatuous figure he had caught a glimpse of in the mirror. Instinctively he turned his back more to the light lest she might see the shame that burned upon his forehead.

The full realization that his wife had all along been dwelling in another world, a world he had never entered and of which he knew nothing, and the utter failure of his irony to bring his wife back to the world of which he, Gabriel, was the center, finally broke the walled circle of his egotism. A dead youth, a mere memory, was the center of the world in which Gretta had all this while been living. As a result of this knowledge, and the way it has been conveyed, Gabriel escapes from himself, as it were, and the rest of the story shows us his expanding consciousness until the point where, dozing off into unconsciousness, he feels a sense of absolute unity, of identity even, with all those elements which before had been hostile to his ego:

> Generous tears filled Gabriel's eyes. . . . The tears gathered more thickly in his eyes and in the partial darkness he imagined he saw the form of a young man standing under a dripping tree. . . . His own identity was fading out into a grey impalpable world: the solid world itself, which these dead had one time reared and lived in, was dissolving and dwindling.
> A few light taps upon the pane made him turn to the window. It had begun to snow again. He watched sleepily the flakes, silver and dark, falling obliquely against the lamplight. The time had come for him to set out on his journey westward. Yes, the newspapers were right: snow was general all over Ireland. It was falling on every part of the dark central plain, on the treeless hills, falling softly upon the bog of Allen and, further westward, softly falling into the dark mutinous Shannon waves. It was falling, too, upon every part of the

lonely churchyard where Michael Furey lay buried. It lay thickly drifted on the crooked crosses and headstones, on the spears of the little gate, on the barren thorns. His soul swooned slowly as he heard the snow falling faintly through the universe and faintly falling, like the descent of their last end, upon all the living and the dead.

The snow, which falls indifferently upon all things, covering them with a neutral whiteness and erasing all their differentiating details, is the symbol of Gabriel's new sense of identity with the world, of the breakdown of the circle of his egotism to allow him to become for the moment not a man different from all other men living in a world of which he alone is the center but a willing part of the general flux of things. The assault, which progressed through so many stages until its final successful stage, had this result, and the contrast with the normal Gabriel is complete.

It is only as a result of some such analysis that the organization and structure of "The Dead" can be seen to be not only effective but inevitable. It is a story which, in the elaborateness of its technique and variations of its prose style (the cadenced inversions of the final passage form a deliberate contrast with the style of the earlier descriptions, adding their share to the presentation of the main theme), stands apart from the others in *Dubliners*. Joyce's versatility is already apparent. "Ivy Day in the Committee Room" has the texture of a Katherine Mansfield story but with a firmness of outline and presentation that Katherine Mansfield lacked in all but two or three of her works. "The Dead" is in a more traditional style, but done with a subtlety and a virtuosity that makes it one of the most remarkable short stories of the present century.

"The Dead" was not part of the original draft of *Dubliners*. It was added later, at a time when Joyce was becoming increasingly preoccupied with the problem of aesthetics. The story is, indeed, a symbolic statement of the aesthetic attitude that he came to accept. Gabriel moves from an egocentric to an impersonal point of view just as the artist (according to Joyce's explanation in A *Portrait of the Artist as a Young Man*) moves from the personal lyrical method to the impersonal dramatic approach. The indifferent acceptance of life as something revolving not round the artist's ego but on its independent axis is for Joyce the ideal aesthetic attitude. Thus "The Dead" is, in some sense, a fable illustrating Joyce's view of the nature of the artist's attitude. It reflects his preoccupation with the problem of defining the aesthetic point of view at this period.

WILLIAM ROSEN

The Presentation of King Lear in Act I, Scene i

It is not absolutely necessary to turn to Elizabethan concepts of kingship or order to understand the respect and honor due to one who is king, who is father, and who is old. Such ideas have not disappeared with the passing of some three hundred and fifty years. However, a brief reference to Elizabethan attitudes is appropriate here because the respect due to Lear is central to the play.

Certainly "kingship" had an evocative power for Elizabethans. There is divinity that hedges a king — we find this idea reiterated in much of the writing of the age. Furthermore, the correspondence between the power of the king and that of the father was an Elizabethan commonplace illustrating the order of a universe in which, as God governed all, so kings ruled states, and fathers, families. In *The French Academie*, whose popularity is attested by its many English editions from 1586 to 1614, La Primaudaye makes an observation that might serve as a commentary on *King Lear*:

> Everie house must be ruled by the eldest, as by a king, who by nature commandeth over everie part of the house, and they obey him for the good preservation thereof. . . . This commandement over children, is called roiall, bicause he that begetteth, commandeth by love, and by the prerogative of age, which is a kind of kingly commanding. . . . The father is the true image of the great & soveraign God, the universal father of al things.

Thus the ordered family, the private life of a nation, is a mirroring in miniature of the ordered hierarchy of public society; and analogies between the king and his subjects and the father and his children prevailed.

It is within such a context that we first see King Lear: his figure activates in the minds of an audience patterns of value of which he is the embodiment. His formal entrance highlights all the dignity and authority associated with kingship. The set of notes sounded, the "sennet," ushers in the concrete symbol of royalty, "enter one bearing a coronet"; and the stage directions give the precise order of entrance which accords with the prerogatives of rank: "King Lear, Cornwall, Albany, Goneril, Regan, Cordelia, and Attendants." On the Elizabethan stage this would be a stately procession of splendor, Lear the central figure in a crowded scene. All are Lear's subjects, dependent on him.

Lear's stature is even further magnified in his first extended pronouncement in which he tells of his intentions to divest himself of "rule,/ Interest of territory, cares of state" (I.i.50), for we see him in the role of public and private figure at one and the same time. Because he is king, his actions in dividing the realm have public consequences affecting the destiny of the state; as benefactor to his children in this division, his actions affect the private life of the family as well. And yet, though the figure of the king bodies forth the ideal, the highest good of family and nation, it is important to see that in this scene Shakespeare presents his central character as an ironist would; and in this way: that the audience does not fully engage its sympathies with Lear or those who oppose him since the dramatist supports the values which Lear represents while revealing the king's misguided position.

Lear's character is objectively dramatized at the beginning. And in situations that are dramatized rather than narrated, the task of projecting states of mind devolves upon the language itself. In Lear's first lengthy speech, which is balanced and regally formal, Shakespeare has the king dramatically reveal himself as proud, authoritative, at the height of his power, wishing to hear not truth, but flattery:

> Tell me, my daughters, —
> Since now we will divest us both of rule,
> Interest of territory, cares of state, —
> Which of you shall we say doth love us most,
> That we our largest bounty may extend
> Where nature doth with merit challenge? Goneril,
> Our eldest-born, speak first.   (I.i.49)

Lear's abdication is thus the occasion for a pageant of flattery: each daughter is to vie with the other in a public display of love. Goneril fulfills his expectations:

> Sir, I love you more than word can wield the matter;
> Dearer than eye-sight, space, and liberty;
> Beyond what can be valued, rich or rare;
> No less than life, with grace, health, beauty, honour;
> As much as child e'er lov'd, or father found;
> A love that makes breath poor, and speech unable:
> Beyond all manner of so much I love you.   (I.i.56)

Shakespeare makes it obvious that Lear already has in mind the kind of answer he expects from his daughters. It is significant that after Goneril's fulsome protestations of love Lear does not evaluate or praise her remarks. He makes no comment at all on her speech. He has heard what he has wanted to hear, and he immediately bestows upon her a share of the kingdom. It is interesting to note that in *The True Chronicle History of King Leir*, when Gonorill proclaims her love for him, Leir comments, "O, how thy words revive my dying soul" (I.iii.54).

Shakespeare reinforces this imperious characteristic of Lear. Again, after Regan's testimony of love, Lear makes no reference to her speech; in *The Chronicle History* he says, "Did never Philomel sing so sweet a note" (I.iii.74). He allots her portion and calls on Cordelia to "Speak." And it is important to observe that in the three instances where Lear asks the daughters to proclaim the extent of their love, he imperiously concludes with the curt, monosyllabic, "Speak." (The Folio omits the concluding "Speak" addressed to Regan.)

Thus, when Cordelia refuses to follow her sisters in answering with "glib and oily art," the stage has been dramatically set for Lear's wrathful indignation.

> *Lear*.   what can you say to draw
>   A third more opulent than your sisters? Speak.
> *Cordelia*. Nothing, my lord.
> *Lear*. Nothing!
> *Cordelia*. Nothing.
> *Lear*. Nothing will come of nothing. Speak again.
> *Cordelia*. Unhappy that I am, I cannot heave
>   My heart into my mouth. I love your Majesty
>   According to my bond; no more nor less.   (I.i.87)

Lear's real attitude comes out when in thwarted rage he reveal-
ingly says to Cordelia: "Better thou/ Hadst not been born than
not t' have pleas'd me better" (I.i.237).

The situation presented here is the problem of any human
relationship: shall we attempt to understand another, really
understand another person, or will we accept him only on our
own terms? Shakespeare presents Lear as a powerful king, wilful
and unyielding, a man who has no desire to understand others
or communicate with them. He has not here the humanity of
thinking beyond himself. He hears only what he wants to hear,
tinting everything with the color of his own mind. When
Cordelia speaks these words:

> Good my lord,
> You have begot me, bred me, lov'd me: I
> Return those duties back as are right fit;
> Obey you, love you, and most honour you.
> Why have my sisters husbands, if they say
> They love you all? Haply, when I shall wed,
> That lord whose hand must take my plight shall carry
> Half my love with them, half my care and duty.
> Sure, I shall never marry like my sisters,
> To love my father all.   (I.i.98)

Lear, expecting an entirely different answer, the kind of satisfying
flattery given by the politic Goneril and Regan, makes no attempt
to understand what Cordelia is really trying to say, and casts off
the person dearest to him.

Though Lear acts in wrathful haste and blindness, his actions
are analyzed, his motivation unfolded, that the audience may see
and understand his character fully and unambiguously. Lear even
explains himself, like an onlooker unfolding the psychology of
action. When he shouts to Cordelia, "Better thou/ Hadst not
been born than not t' have pleas'd me better" (I.i.237), he is,
in a way, impartially describing himself as one who values love
only as a means of adding to his own vanity. And in Kent's
banishment there is the same self-revelation. In violent outburst
Lear says that Kent must be banished because he sought to make
the king break his vow and reverse his sentence which "nor our
nature nor our place can bear" (I.i.174). Yet such statements
cannot be taken as indications of a high degree of self-awareness
on the part of the protagonist. They are best viewed as a mode of

partial narrative which S. L. Bethell has described as "appropriate to poetic drama, since it renders the psychological situation clear without transferring attention from the verse to the process of naturalistic induction."

One can say that in the beginning Lear equates "nature" with his own "conception" of himself; that for Lear the natural rights inherent in majesty, fatherhood, and age demand — or, rather, take for granted — the unquestioning and undivided love of children for parent, benefactor and king; the respect of youth for age; and the complete obedience of subject to ruler. Thus, when Cordelia refuses to conform to Lear's own conception of what is natural, the king arbitrarily casts her off as unnatural, disclaiming all "paternal care,/ Propinquity and property of blood" (I.i.115). He banishes Kent because his "nature" allows not the breaking of vows. For Lear, then, nature is not the external world, or reason, but his own image; and he looks out onto a world which must mirror back his own conceptions of loyalty, love, justice, perfection. Proudly independent in the omnipotence of self, he is detached from all, and in his isolation feels no responsibility and kinship towards others. Lear's folly, like that of Oedipus, is one of blindness, the overweening belief in the infallibility of one's own being, the failure to recognize the limitations of mortality.

To characterize Lear's folly as anything but the result of misguided intellect is to reduce his stature and worth, and turn him into a pathetic figure, as Lamb's version of a "painful and disgusting" spectacle, "an old man tottering about the stage with a walking-stick, turned out of doors by his daughters in a rainy night"; or Lily B. Campbell's version of Lear as "the slave of habitual wrath"; or the very extreme view of G. W. Knight who pictured Lear as the supreme pathetic figure of literature because of his "puerile intellect."

That Lear has no true insight into himself, his actions, and those about him can, on analysis, be seen as the leitmotif of the opening scene. The loyal Kent draws attention to the problem of appearance versus reality when he says to Lear:

> Thy youngest daughter does not love thee least;
> Nor are those empty-hearted whose low sounds
> Reverb no hollowness.   (I.i.154)

Certainly hollowness is Kent's judgment of Goneril and Regan, a pointed reference to their earlier professions of love. Notice the abstractions that Goneril used when she affirmed her love to be dearer than space, liberty, life, grace, health, beauty, honor. In his blind pride Lear has been deceived by the world of appearances; he mistakes the outward appearance of Goneril and Regan, their veneer of words which cover the evil within them, for the real, sincere and speechless love of Cordelia. As has often been noticed, a similar situation exists in Sophocles' *Oedipus Rex* where Oedipus is at first blind to the realities of the world in which he lives. The prophet who was blind, Tiresias, saw; and the king who saw was blind.

When the bluntly speaking Kent, who sees true relations and is not deceived by appearances, is banished with Lear's words echoing, "Out of my sight," he replies, "See better, Lear," — an exhortation which is given further significance at the end of the scene when Regan tells Goneril that the king "hath ever but slenderly known himself" (I.i.296). And when Lear's explosive, "now, by Apollo, —" is picked up by Kent, "Now, by Apollo, king,/ Thou swear'st thy gods in vain" (I.i.162), it is an ironic comment on the king's inability to distinguish true value, the faithful Cordelia and Kent, from mere appearance, the seemingly dutiful Goneril and Regan. It is to be remembered that Apollo was the god of light, and that inscribed on the temple of Apollo at Delphi was the famous "Know Thyself." Also inscribed there was the injunction "Nothing in Excess."

The first scene presents us with the basic facts of the play: the division of kingdom, the scorning of the faithful Cordelia and Kent. Shakespeare gives the audience a point of view towards the hero of the play: through Lear's own speech and actions we see him as proudly blind and regal; and this view is substantiated for us by Lear's friend, Kent, and by his future antagonists, Goneril and Regan. These three appraise him and reach the same conclusions. Kent slightingly calls him "old man," characterizes his actions as "folly" and "hideous rashness." At the end of the scene, when Goneril and Regan review the happenings in businesslike prose, their final judgment of the king, shrewd and incisive, has already been dramatized as truth:

> *Goneril.* You see how full of changes his age is; the observation we have made of it hath not been little. He always lov'd our sister most; and with what poor judgement he hath now cast her off appears too grossly.
>
> *Regan.* 'Tis the infirmity of his age; yet he hath ever but slenderly known himself.

> Goneril. The best and soundest of his time hath been but rash; then
> must we look from his age to receive not alone the imperfections
> of long-engraffed condition, but therewithal the unruly wayward-
> ness that infirm and choleric years bring with them.   (I.i.291)

The speeches of Goneril and Regan at the end of this exposition
scene attune us to their later treatment of Lear by arousing a
state of expectation, of speculation as to how they will curb their
father and king, who has given up his power and yet would, as
Goneril fears, still "manage those authorities/ That he hath
given away!" (I.iii.17)

In analyzing the way in which Shakespeare portrays Lear at
the beginning of the play it becomes evident that the audience
sees and understands events not primarily through Lear's eyes,
thus becoming one with him, sympathizing with his actions, but
through the eyes of Kent and Goneril and Regan who interpret
him for us. Friend and foes, by agreeing on the folly which impels
Lear, formulate a dramatic attitude towards the character.

JOSEPH WOOD KRUTCH

Moral Vision in Arthur Miller and Tennessee Williams

Neither Miller's *Death of a Salesman* nor Tennessee Williams'
A Streetcar Named Desire is a cheerful play. Both end with what
looks less like a tragic affirmation than like a simple confession
of defeat. Neither Willy Loman nor Blanche Dubois is likely to
strike the spectator as a very dignified or very noble character,
and both are completely destroyed — as, say, Hamlet and Othello
are not completely destroyed — when the story ends. Loman is
a suicide and Blanche is being led away to a madhouse.

Obviously neither Miller nor Williams plainly commits himself as do Maxwell Anderson and O'Neill to either the form or
the ethical content of classic tragedy. Moreover, neither exhibits
as plainly as it seems to me O'Neill exhibits, a determination to
seek persistently for something in the universe outside man to
which he can appeal and "belong." It is possible to interpret
Death of a Salesman as brutal naturalism and *A Streetcar Named
Desire* as a sort of semi-surrealist version of the Strindbergian sub-
mission to destructive obsessions.

Reprinted from *"Modernism" in Modern Drama* by Joseph Wood
Krutch by permission of the author. (The title of this essay is the
editor's.)

If such is a proper summation, then Miller and Williams, the two most widely discussed American playwrights of the moment, follow O'Neill and Anderson only as Sean O'Casey followed Synge. They represent, that is to say, the collapse of a reaction and illustrate, as did O'Casey, an irresistible pull in the direction of nihilism and despair.

Perhaps, indeed, that is the proper interpretation to be put upon their work and their current popularity. I am unwilling, however, to leave the subject without suggesting the possibility that there may be something to be said on the other side, and at the risk of being accused of overinterpretation, I should like to say it.

So far as *Death of a Salesman* is concerned, it seems reasonable to suppose that it is intended as something a little more than merely detached "scientific" naturalism. Most spectators, I think, assume that it embodies some "social criticism," and most, I imagine, assume that the social criticism is of a sort by now very traditional. In this view, Willy Loman is the victim of an unjust competitive society. He was first corrupted by its false ideals and then exploited by those shrewder and more ruthless than himself. Society made him what he was, and in a better society his fate would have been a happier one. In all this there is, of course, nothing incompatible with what I have been loosely calling "modernism." The doctrine and methods of the naturalists lend themselves very readily to such "social significance."

What makes it impossible to dismiss *Death of a Salesman* as merely left-wing naturalism is the curious fact that Miller himself seems to be some sort of pluralist and that his play could be interpreted, not as a demonstration of the workings of social determinism, but as a study of the effects of moral weakness and irresponsibility. Willy Loman is a victim of society, but he is also a victim of himself. He accepted an essentially vulgar and debased as well as a false system of values. He himself says, and the audience seems to be expected to believe him, that he might have led a happy life if he had followed his own bent and become, for example, a carpenter, instead of submitting to the prejudice which makes a salesman more respectable than a man who works with his hands. His tragic guilt — and it is his, not society's — was, in this view, a very old-fashioned one. He was not true to himself. Thus the moral of the play becomes a classical moral and must necessarily presume both the existence of the classical ego and the power to make a choice.

Seen in this light, Miller becomes a moralist, at least in the sense and in much the same fashion that Ibsen was still a moralist. He has found his way back along the road which leads to determinism and the disappearance of the ego at least to the point where the dramatic disciples of Ibsen first entered upon it, and *Death of a Salesman* thus becomes a qualified reaffirmation of the individual's privilege of being, within certain limits, what he chooses to be.

The case of Tennessee Williams is different but equally dubious. As I have already suggested, the most obvious interpretations put him plainly among the despairing explorers of pathological states of mind just as the obvious interpretations put Arthur Miller among the sociological naturalists. In all his most striking plays, *The Glass Menagerie, Summer and Smoke*, and *A Streetcar Named Desire*, the chief character is obsessed, and in the last two the obsession takes a sexual form. Madness seems to interest the author more than anything else, and at least in the third and most successful of the plays a quasi-expressionist technique is used for the purpose of persuading the audience to see certain of the events from the standpoint of the heroine's abnormality rather than from its own presumably objective point of view.

In each of the three plays there is another recurrent theme. Each of the heroines numbers among her obsessions the fact that she is or was "a lady." In each the ideal of respectability, the sense that her parents and her remoter ancestors lived in accordance with some code to which she herself would like to be loyal but which no one with whom she comes in contact acknowledges, is so strong as to appear crucial. In *The Glass Menagerie* the mother sees her family disintegrating because it no longer finds her dream of respectability anything but annoying. In both *Summer and Smoke* and *A Streetcar Named Desire* the heroine seems to succumb to crude sexuality because she has so fanatically refused to accept a normal life among people who appear to her as hopelessly unrefined.

Tennessee Williams grew up in the South. Like so many other Southern writers, the existence of a decayed aristocracy was one of the inescapable facts of the society with which he was most familiar. That representatives of such a decayed aristocracy should appear in his plays may mean no more than that they were part of his experience. Nevertheless it seems to me obvious that hi persistent concern with them does have a greater significance. These helpless survivors from the past, feeble and pathetic clingers to a dead tradition, take on the importance of symbols. They are not accidental facts; they mean something.

Upon the answer to the question "What do they mean? Of what are they symbols?" depends the whole meaning of the plays so far as our own special theme is concerned. Let us consider it in connection with *A Streetcar Named Desire*.

Blanche DuBois, a decayed aristocrat and a fanatical lady, has already lost her position as a schoolteacher because she is also a nymphomaniac. As the curtain rises we see her arriving alone and seeking refuge in the squalid home of her sister Stella, who has married a crude and brutal young man of foreign extraction. This sister has made what the psychologists would call "a satisfactory adjustment." She has rejected and forgotten the traditions of her past. She has accepted the frank squalor of her surroundings and the ignorant brutality of her husband, chiefly because she is reveling delightedly in his abundant and animalistic sexuality. Blanche, the nymphomaniac, is horrified by what some would call her sister's "normality." She makes a feeble and ridiculous attempt to instruct both the sister and her husband in the genteel tradition, and she is violently repelled by their contented animality. But because she can neither lead their life nor the genteel life of which she dreams, her last defenses crumble and she is led away to an asylum, certifiably insane.

Everything depends upon, as the phrase goes, which side the author is on. It appears that to many members of the audience this question presents no difficulty. They are, and they assume that the author is, on the side of the sister. She is "healthy," "adjusted," "normal." She lives in the present; she accepts things as they are; and she will never be confined to a madhouse. Her husband is crude, even somewhat brutal, but he is also virile; he is the natural man and one of literature's many kinsmen of Lady Chatterley's lover. Virility, even orgiastic virility, is the proper answer to decadence. Stella, the representative of a decayed aristocracy, is rejuvenated by a union with a representative of "the people."

Even more conspicuously than in the case of Arthur Miller's play, an alternate reading of the situation is possible. In Miller one suspects a sort of pluralism. In Williams the question presents itself instead under the form of an ambiguity.

By this I mean that while one section of the audience takes the side of Stella almost as a matter of course another section understands and shares Blanche's revulsion. Her instincts are right. She is on the side of civilization and refinement. But the age has placed her in a tragic dilemma. She looks about for a tradition according to which she may live and a civilization to which she can be loyal. She finds none. Ours is a society which has lost its shape.

Behind her lies a past which, at least in retrospect, seems to have been civilized. The culture of the Old South is dead, and she has good reason to know that it is. It is, however, the only culture about which she knows anything. The world of Stella and of her husband is a barbarism, — perhaps, as its admirers would say, a vigorous barbarism — but a barbarism nonetheless. Blanche chooses the dead past and becomes the victim of that impossible choice. But she does choose it rather than the "adjustment" of her sister. At least she has not succumbed to barbarism.

As I have said, one's choice of sides will depend largely upon one's attitude toward Stella's "virile" husband. The real question is whether he is villain or hero. If we knew which he is to his creator, we should know whether Williams should be classified among that group of "moderns" who see in a return to the primitive the possible rejuvenation of mankind or whether he belongs rather with traditionalists, such as the esoteric T. S. Eliot on the one hand or the popular Maxwell Anderson on the other, who maintain that from the past itself we shall still have to learn if we are ever to learn at all what civilization means.

I cannot tell you what Williams thinks or says. I can, after due warning, report a very significant thing which he is said to have said. At third hand I have it that when queried in conversation about the meaning of A *Streetcar Named Desire*, or rather about the significance of its chief male character, he replied: "It means that if you do not watch out the apes will take over."

If this report is accurate, and I repeat that I have it only at third hand, the question is answered. Williams, despite all the violence of his plays, despite what sometimes looks very much like nihilism, is really on the side of what modernists would call the Past rather than the Future — which means, of course on the side of those who believe that the future, if there is to be any civilized future, will be less new than most modern dramatists from Ibsen on have professed to believe.

MARK VAN DOREN

Wordsworth's "The Solitary Reaper"

WILLIAM WORDSWORTH

The Solitary Reaper

Behold her, single in the field,
 Yon solitary Highland lass!
Reaping and singing by herself;
 Stop here, or gently pass!
Alone she cuts and binds the grain,   5
And sings a melancholy strain;
O listen! for the vale profound
Is overflowing with the sound.

No nightingale did ever chaunt
 More welcome notes to weary bands   10
Of travelers in some shady haunt,
 Among Arabian sands:
A voice so thrilling ne'er was heard
In spring-time from the cuckoo-bird,
Breaking the silence of the seas   15
Among the farthest Hebrides.

Will no one tell me what she sings? —
 Perhaps the plaintive numbers flow
For old, unhappy, far-off things,
 And battles long ago: 20
Or is it some more humble lay,
Familiar matter of today?
Some natural sorrow, loss, or pain,
That has been, and may be again?

Whate'er the theme, the maiden sang   25
 As if her song could have no ending;
I saw her singing at her work,
 And o'er the sickle bending; —
I listened, motionless and still;
And, as I mounted up the hill,   30
The music in my heart I bore,
Long after it was heard no more.

From *Introduction to Poetry* by Mark Van Doren. Copyright, 1951, by William Sloane Associates, Inc. Copyright © 1966 by Mark Van Doren. Reprinted by permission of Hill and Wang, Inc. (The title of this essay is the editor's.)

The fact that this poem is not equally good in all of its parts does not mean that it is unadmirable. Perhaps no poem is perfect or could be; and perhaps an appearance of perfection is the most suspicious appearance a poem can put up. At any rate, here is a famous poem that deserves its fame, and yet each stanza is inferior to the one before it. The first, which is the best, has none before it, and in fact contains or expresses the whole of the impulse that was moving Wordsworth as he wrote. Not as he saw this Highland girl, for he never saw her. He read about her in a prose book of travels, Thomas Wilkinson's *Tour in Scotland*. Wilkinson saw the solitary lass, and wrote a sentence about her which made Wordsworth in effect see her too — made him, that is, see her as a poet. Many great poems have come thus out of books: most commonly, out of prose books. Prose discovers the matter and leaves it clear; after which the poet has only to write his poem as if the matter of it were his own, as indeed it comes to be.

Wordsworth is most deeply interested in the fact that this girl in his mind's eye inhabits a solitude. It is not the solitude of Pound, Whitman, or Peele. There are many solitudes, and the present one is Wordsworth's own of which he always wrote so well. He puts the reaper into it and makes her belong there, a figure undefined except by the fact that she stands alone in a world which has no content other than her thought and feeling. Her mood at the moment is melancholy in the sweet way that Wordsworth understood so well. Good and healthy persons, in harmony with their surroundings, are both sad and happy there. They do not comprehend their universe as it weighs upon them, but they love it and can therefore bear its weight — gravely, because it is so huge and old, but joyfully too because they feel their strength as they do so.

The first eight lines say all that Wordsworth really has to say about this, and about the girl who is his symbol. "Behold her, single in the field." She is single; she is solitary; she is by herself; she is alone — we are told four times, in five lines, that this is true, as if nothing else matters, and nothing does for Wordsworth. Also, she is singing. She is a peasant girl, and she is singing as her kind is disposed to do, sadly, sweetly, and powerfully to herself. The folk knows, if civilized men do not, how the weight of the world is borne by those whose turn has come to be alive in it. Such is Wordsworth's deepest conviction as in his

imagination he watches the girl. The eight lines put her clearly
before us, bending gracefully as she sings some song of which
he says only that it is melancholy, and that it is loud enough
to fill a whole valley.

> O listen! for the vale profound
> Is overflowing with the sound.

If these are the best lines in the poem, the reason is their mysterious power to create the thing they mention. The deep valley
fills with music as we listen; and overflows. This is partly a matter
of onomatopoeia in the lines themselves, and partly a matter of
their rhythmical relation to the six lines above. The eight-line
stanza Wordsworth has decided to use — perhaps he is deciding
only now — consists of a quatrain and two couplets. To point
this out is not to explain the force we feel in the series as
Wordsworth manages it. Few poems have begun more happily,
or so rapidly achieved so much momentum. The initial quatrain,
tetrameter except for its short fourth line which so sensibly halts
us for a scrutiny of the thing, the person to be seen — the girl
herself, bending down and rising up, reaping and soliloquizing —
is followed, once we have checked our progress and stopped to
gaze, by two melodious pairs of lines whose rhymes flow into one
another as if by magic, producing in us a lively sense of the music
which takes its rise in the maiden, fills the valley around her,
keeps on filling it, and overflows. The two couplets are in a sense
one sound, drawn out indefinitely and continuing in our ears,
so that the remainder of the poem, no matter what it may say,
will be assured of an accompaniment, a ground harmony, a
remembered song that hums in the mind long after its occasion
has ceased.

Having done this much — and it was a great thing to do —
Wordsworth henceforth is reduced to conscious reflection upon
his subject. The reflections are fine and the poem as a whole is
fine, but nothing in it, not even the second stanza, quite matches
that opening section in which the subject was created — all at
once created, by no effort that could be observed, and by no
means that we may be altogether sure of naming rightly.

The first reflection takes the form of a comparison. The song
we heard was beautiful and strong; there is no doubt of that; but
Wordsworth must suspect us of doubt, or he would not tell us
how much better it was than something else. Than the voice of

the Arabian nightingale; or the voice of the cuckoo in spring,
among the farthest Hebrides. South or north, he insists, there is
nothing to compare; and yet the comparison proceeds. The fact
that it is a double comparison does not help to justify it. The
girl's song is said to be more exciting than either of two distant
sounds; and we believe this, yet are left thinking of those distant
sounds, which replace hers. The second of them in particular is
rendered with genius. The two compound words in line 14,
"spring-time" and "cuckoo-bird," reinforce each other so freshly
that one of them seems to spring out of the other as a rocket
springs out of itself, bounding off with redoubled speed and joy.
In two strokes of its wings the line mounts high and flies away,
taking us with it to remote and moveless seas which nevertheless
tremble when this sound arrives. "Breaking" is the word. It
creates the very silence it shatters, softly and far away.

The stanza is noble, yet less so than the one that rendered it
unnecessary. And the rest of the poem goes steadily downhill.
The third stanza is of all things a rhetorical question, or worse
yet, a pair of them. "Will no one tell me what she sings?" Certainly no one will, for Wordsworth is the authority. He does
not understand these Highland words, or the girl is too far away
for them to be heard, but that is no matter. The net meaning
of the song is his to know if anybody is to know it, and he should
not be asking for assistance. Lines 18–20 are agreeably suggestive
of a romantic burden which the words may bear; and as such
they are preferable to the couplets (21–24) he dutifully writes
because he remembers his own theory that great poetry comes
out of familiar and domestic things as well as out of battles long
ago; it is not a useful theory at the moment, but he jogs on
through it, finishing the stanza at last. He has long since lost
contact with his subject in its purity. The quatrain of this stanza
was intrinsically better than its couplets; but it was in the
quatrain that he strayed away, farther even than he had gone in
the magnificent stanza about the sands of Arabia and the Hebridean seas.

The last stanza recovers a fragment of the magic that is gone,
but only a fragment. "Whate'er the theme" — it begins prosaically, still reflecting upon a very unimportant topic. It moves
then into a series of lines whose function is to fix in us a sense of
the song's immortality. We had that sense at the end of the first
stanza, and noted it then. There is no object to our being re
minded of it at the end of the poem — the poem, Wordsworth

seems to be saying, will end but the song will not — and yet there is little chance that we shall be excited by learning something we already know. Wordsworth throws his discourse into the past tense — "I saw her," "I listened" — but this is a mere device of syntax. "I listened, motionless and still." That is better, for it suspends both him and us in a state of listening where it is possible to lose ourselves. This had been, however, our original state, which the second and third stanzas interrupted; and perhaps it is not available to us again. Indeed it is not, or to Wordsworth either, judging by the pious assurance he gives us in the last three lines that he will not forget an unforgettable experience. The experience, in fact, is dead; though we can always revive it by returning and rereading stanza one. That is the contribution of the poem, and it alone makes the entire work admirable.

JOHN CIARDI

Robert Frost: The Way to the Poem

ROBERT FROST

Stopping by Woods on a Snowy Evening

Whose woods these are I think I know.
His house is in the village though;
He will not see me stopping here
To watch his woods fill up with snow.

My little horse must think it queer
To stop without a farmhouse near
Between the wood and frozen lake
The darkest evening of the year.

He gives his harness bells a shake
To ask if there is some mistake.
The only other sound's the sweep
Of easy wind and downy flake.

The woods are lovely, dark and deep.
But I have promises to keep,
And miles to go before I sleep,
And miles to go before I sleep.

The School System has much to say these days of the virtue of reading widely, and not enough about the virtues of reading less but in depth. There are any number of reading lists for poetry, but there is not enough talk about individual poems. Poetry, finally, is one poem at a time. To read any one poem carefully is the ideal preparation for reading another. Only a poem can illustrate how poetry works.

Above, therefore, is a poem — one of the master lyrics of the English language, and almost certainly the best-known poem by an American poet. What happens in it? — which is to say, not *what* does it mean, but *how* does it mean? How does it go about being a human re-enactment of a human experience? The author — perhaps the thousandth reader would need to be told — is Robert Frost.

Even the TV audience can see that this poem begins as a seemingly simply narration of a seemingly simple incident but ends by suggesting meanings far beyond anything specifically referred to in the narrative. And even readers with only the most casual interest in poetry might be made to note the additional fact that, though the poem suggests those larger meanings, it is very careful never to abandon its pretense to being simply narration. There is duplicity at work. The poet pretends to be talking about one thing, and all the while he is talking about many others.

Many readers are forever unable to accept the poet's essential duplicity. It is almost safe to say that a poem is never about what it seems to be about. As much could be said of the proverb. The bird in the hand, the rolling stone, the stitch in time never (except by an artful double deception) intend any sort of statement about birds, stones, or sewing. The incident of this poem, one must conclude, is at root a metaphor.

Duplicity aside, this poem's movement from the specific to the general illustrates one of the basic formulas of all poetry. Such a grand poem as Arnold's "Dover Beach" and such lesser, though unfortunately better-known, poems as Longfellow's "Village Blacksmith" and Holmes's "Chambered Nautilus" are built on the same progression. In these three poems, however, the generalization is markedly set apart from the specific narration, and even seems additional to the telling rather than intrinsic to it. It is this sense of division one has in mind in speaking of "a tacked-on moral."

There is nothing wrong-in-itself with a tacked-on moral. Frost, in fact, makes excellent use of the device at times. In this poem, however, Frost is careful to let the whatever-the-moral-is grow out of the poem itself. When the action ends the poem ends. There is no epilogue and no explanation. Everything pretends to be about the narrated incident. And that pretense sets the basic tone of the poem's performance of itself.

The dramatic force of that performance is best observable, I believe, as a progression in three scenes.

In scene one, which coincides with stanza one, a man — a New England man — is driving his sleigh somewhere at night. It is snowing, and as the man passes a dark patch of woods he stops to watch the snow descend into the darkness. We know, moreover, that the man is familiar with these parts (he knows who owns the woods and where the owner lives), and we know that no one has seen him stop. As scene one forms itself in the theatre of the mind's-eye, therefore, it serves to establish some as yet unspecified relation between the man and the woods.

It is necessary, however, to stop here for a long parenthesis: Even so simple an opening statement raises any number of questions. It is impossible to address all the questions that rise from the poem stanza by stanza, but two that arise from stanza one illustrate the sort of thing one might well ask of the poem detail by detail.

Why, for example, does the man not say what errand he is on? What is the force of leaving the errand generalized? He might just as well have told us that he was going to the general store, or returning from it with a jug of molasses he had promised to bring Aunt Harriet and two suits of long underwear he had promised to bring the hired man. Frost, moreover, can handle homely detail to great effect. He preferred to leave his motive generalized. Why ?

And why, on the other hand, does he say so much about knowing the absent owner of the woods and where he lives? Is it simply that one set of details happened in whereas another did not? To speak of things "happening in" is to assault the integrity of a poem. Poetry cannot be discussed meaningfully unless one can assume that everything in the poem — every last comma and variant spelling — is in it by the poet's specific act of choice. Only bad poets allow into their poems what is haphazard or cheaply chosen.

The errand, I will venture a bit brashly for lack of space, is left generalized in order the more aptly to suggest *any* errand in life and, therefore, life itself. The owner is there because he is one of the forces of the poem. Let it do to say that the force he represents is the village of mankind (that village at the edge of winter) from which the poet finds himself separated (has separated himself?) in his moment by the woods (and to which, he recalls finally, he has promises to keep). The owner is he-who-lives-in-his-village-house, thereby locked away from the poet's awareness of the-time-the-snow-tells as it engulfs and obliterates the world the village man allows himself to believe he "owns." Thus, the owner is a representative of an order of reality from which the poet has divided himself for the moment, though to a certain extent he ends by reuniting with it. Scene one, therefore, establishes not only a relation between the man and the woods, but the fact that the man's relation begins with his separation (though momentarily) from mankind.

End parenthesis one, begin parenthesis two.

Still considering the first scene as a kind of dramatic performance of forces, one must note that the poet has meticulously matched the simplicity of his language to the pretended simplicity of the narrative. Clearly, the man stopped because the beauty of the scene moved him, but he neither tells us that the scene is beautiful nor that he is moved. A bad writer, always ready to overdo, might have written: "The vastness gripped me, filling my spirit with the slow steady sinking of the snow's crystalline perfection into the glimmerless profundities of the hushed primeval wood." Frost's avoidance of such a spate illustrates two principles of good writing. The first, he has stated himself in "The Mowing": "Anything *more* than the truth would have seemed too weak" (italics mine). Understatement is one of the basic sources of power in English poetry. The second principle is to let the action speak for itself. A good novelist does not tell us that a given character is good or bad (at least not since the passing of the Dickens tradition): he shows us the character in action, and then, watching him, we know. Poetry, too, has fictional obligations: even when the characters are ideas and metaphors rather than people, they must be *characterized in action*. A poem does not *talk about* ideas; it *enacts* them. The force of the poem's performance, in fact, is precisely to act out (and thereby to make us act out emphatically, that is, to *feel out*, that is, *to identify with*) the speaker and why he stopped. The man is the principle actor in this little "drama of why," and in scene one he is the only character, though, as noted, he is somehow related to the absent owner.

End second parenthesis.

In scene two (stanzas two and three) a *foil* is introduced. In fiction and drama, a foil is a character who "plays against" a more important character. By presenting a different point of view or an opposed set of motives, the foil moves the more important character to react in ways that might not have found expression without such opposition. The more important character is thus more fully revealed — to the reader and to himself. The foil here is the horse.

The horse forces the question. Why did the man stop? Until it occurs to him that his "little horse must think it queer" he had not asked himself for reasons. He had simply stopped. But the man finds himself faced with the question he imagines the horse to be asking: what *is* there to stop for out there in the cold, away from bin and stall (house and village and mankind?) and all that any self-respecting beast could value on such a night? In sensing that other view, the man is forced to examine his own more deeply.

In stanza two the question arises only as a feeling within the man. In stanza three, however (still scene two), the horse acts. He gives his harness bells a shake. "What's wrong?" he seems to say. "What are we waiting for?"

By now, obviously, the horse — without losing its identity as horse — has also become a symbol. A symbol is something that stands for something else. Whatever that something else may be, it certainly begins as that order of life that does not understand why a man stops in the wintry middle of nowhere to watch the snow come down. (Can one fail to sense by now that the dark and the snowfall symbolize a death wish, however momentary, *i.e.*, that hunger for final rest and surrender that a man may feel, but not a beast?

So by the end of scene two the performance has given dramatic force to three elements that work upon the man. There is his relation to the world of the owner. There is his relation to the brute world of the horse. And there is also that third presence of the unownable world, the movement of the all-engulfing snow across all the orders of life, the man's, the owners, and the horse's — with the difference that the man knows of that second dark-within-the-dark of which the horse cannot, and the owner will not, know.

The man ends scene two with all these forces working upon him simultaneously. He feels himself moved to a decision. And he feels a last call from the darkness: "the sweep / Of easy wind and downy flake." It would be so easy and so downy to go into the woods and let himself be covered over.

But scene three (stanza four) produces a fourth force. This fourth force can be given many names. It is certainly better, in fact, to give it many names than to attempt to limit it to one. It is social obligation, or personal commitment, or duty, or just the realization that a man cannot indulge a mood forever. All of these and more. But, finally, he has a simple decision to make. He may go into the woods and let the darkness and the snow swallow him from the world of beast and man. Or he must move on. And unless he is going to stop here forever, it is time to remember that he has a long way to go and that he had best be getting there. (So there is something to be said for the horse, too.)

Then and only then, his question driven more and more deeply into himself by these cross-forces, does the man venture a comment on what attracted him: "The woods are lovely, dark and deep." His mood lingers over the thought of that lovely dark-and-deep (as do the very syllables in which he phrases the thought), but the final decision is to put off the mood and move on. He has his man's way to go and his man's obligations to tend to before he can yield. He has miles to go before his sleep. He repeats that thought and the performance ends.

But why the repetition? The first time Frost says "And miles to go before I sleep," there can be little doubt that the primary meaning is: "I have a long way to go before I get to bed tonight." The second time he says it, however, "miles to go" and "sleep" are suddenly transformed into symbols. What are those "something-elses" the symbols stand for? Hundreds of people have tried to ask Mr. Frost that question and he has always turned it away. He has turned it away *because he cannot answer it.* He could answer some part of it. But some part is not enough.

For a symbol is like a rock dropped into a pool: it sends out ripples in all directions, and the ripples are in motion. Who can say where the last ripple disappears? One may have a sense that he knows the approximate center point of the ripples, the point at which the stone struck the water. Yet even then he has trouble marking it surely. How does one make a mark on water? Oh very well — the center point of that second "miles to go" is probably approximately in the neighborhood of being close to meaning, perhaps, "the road of life"; and the second "before I sleep" is maybe that close to meaning "before I take my final rest," the rest in darkness that seemed so temptingly dark-and-deep for the moment of the mood. But the ripples continue to move and the light to change on the water, and the longer one watches the more changes he sees. Such shifting-and-being-at-the-same-instant is of the very sparkle and life of poetry. One experiences it as one experiences life, for every time he looks at an experience he sees something new, and he sees it change as he watches it. And that sense of continuity in fluidity is one of the primary kinds of knowledge, one of man's basic ways of knowing, and one that only the arts can teach, poetry foremost among them.

Frost himself certainly did not ask what that repeated last line meant. It came to him and he received it. He "felt right" about it. And what he "felt right" about was in no sense a "meaning" that, say, an essay could apprehend, but an act of experience that could be fully presented only by the dramatic enactment of forces which is the performance of the poem.

Now look at the poem in another way. Did Frost know what he was going to do when he began? Considering the poem simply as an act of skill, as a piece of juggling, one cannot fail to respond to the magnificent turn at the end where, with one flip, seven of the simplest words in the language suddenly dazzle full of never-ending waves of thought and feeling. Or, more precisely, of felt-thought. Certainly an equivalent stunt by a juggler — could there be an equivalent — would bring the house down. Was it to cap his performance with that grand stunt that Frost wrote the poem?

Far from it. The obvious fact is that *Frost could not have known he was going to write those lines until he wrote them.* Then a second fact must be registered: *he wrote them because, for the fun of it, he had got himself into trouble.*

Frost, like every good poet, began by playing a game with himself. The most usual way of writing a four-line stanza with four feet to the line is to rhyme the third line with the first, and the fourth line with the second. Even that much rhyme is so difficult in English that many poets and almost all of the anonymous ballad makers do not bother to rhyme the first and third lines at all, settling for two rhymes in four lines as good enough. For English is a rhyme-poor language. In Italian and in French, for example, so many words end with the same sounds that rhyming is relatively easy — so easy that many modern French and Italian poets do not bother to rhyme at all. English, being a more agglomerate language, has far more final sounds, hence fewer of them rhyme. When an Italian poet writes a line ending with "vita" (life) he has literally hundreds of rhyme choices available. When an English poet writes "life" at the end of a line he can summon "strife, wife, knife, fife, rife," and then he is in trouble. Now "life-strife" and "life-rife" and "life-wife" seem to offer a combination of possible ideas that can be related by more than just the rhyme. Inevitably, therefore, the poets have had to work and rework these combinations until the sparkle has gone out of them. The reader is normally tired of such rhyme-led associations. When he encounters "life-strife" he is certainly entitled to suspect that the poet did not really want to say "strife" — that had there been in English such a word as, say, "hife," meaning "infinite peace and harmony," the poet would as gladly have used that word instead of "strife." Thus, the reader feels that the writing is haphazard, that the rhyme is making the poet say things he does not really feel, and which, therefore, the reader does not feel except as boredom. One likes to see the rhymes fall into place, but he must end with the belief that it is the poet who is deciding what is said and not the rhyme scheme that is forcing the saying.

So rhyme is a kind of game, and an especially difficult one in English. As in every game, the fun of the rhyme is to set one's difficulties high and then to meet them skilfully. As Frost himself once defined it, freedom consists of "moving easy in harness."

In "Stopping by Woods on a Snowy Evening" Frost took a chance. He decided to rhyme not two lines in each stanza, but three. Not even Frost could have sustained that much rhyme in a long poem (as Dante, for example, with the advantage of writing in Italian, sustained triple rhyme for thousands of lines in *The Divine Comedy*). Frost would have known instantly, therefore, when he took the original chance, that he was going to write a short poem. He would have had that much foretaste of it.

So the first stanza emerged a-a-b-a. And with the sure sense that this was to be a short poem, Frost decided to take an additional chance and to redouble: in English three rhymes in four lines is more than enough; there is no need to rhyme the fourth line. For the fun of it, however, Frost set himself to pick up that loose rhyme and to weave it into the pattern, thereby accepting the all but impossible burden of quadruple rhyme.

The miracle is that it worked. Despite the enormous freight of rhyme, the poem not only came out as a neat pattern, but managed to do so with no sense of strain. Every word and every rhyme falls into place as naturally and as inevitably as if there were no rhyme restricting the poet's choices.

That ease-in-difficulty is certainly inseparable from the success of the poem's performance. One watches the skill-man juggle three balls, then four, then five, and every addition makes the trick more wonderful. But unless he makes the hard trick seem as easy as an easy trick, then all is lost.

The real point, however, is not only that Frost took on a hard rhyme-trick and made it seem easy. It is rather as if the juggler, carried away, had tossed up one more ball than he could really handle, and then amazed himself by actually handling it. So with the real triumph of this poem. Frost could not have known what a stunning effect his repetition of the last line was going to produce. He could not even know he was going to repeat the line. He simply found himself up against a difficulty he almost certainly had not foreseen and he had to improvise to meet it. For in picking up the rhyme from the third line of stanza one and carrying it over into stanza two, he had created an endless chain-link form within which each stanza left a hook sticking out for the next stanza to hang on. So by stanza four, feeling the poem rounding to its end, Frost had to do something about that extra rhyme.

He might have tucked it back into a third line rhyming with the *know-though-snow* of stanza one. He could thus have rounded the poem out to the mathematical symmetry of using each rhyme four times. But though such a device might be defensible in theory, a rhyme repeated after eleven lines is so far from its original rhyme sound that its feeling as rhyme must certainly be lost. And what good is theory if the reader is not moved by the writing?

It must have been in some such quandary that the final repetition suggested itself — a suggestion born of the very difficulties the poet had let himself in for. So there is that point beyond mere ease in handling a hard thing, the point at which the very difficulty offers the poet the opportunity to do better than he knew he could. What, aside from having that happen to oneself, could be more self-delighting than to participate in its happening by one's reader-identification with the poem?

And by now a further point will have suggested itself: that the human insight of the poem and the technicalities of its poetic artifice are inseparable. Each feeds the other. That interplay is the poem's meaning, a matter not of WHAT DOES IT MEAN, for no one can ever say entirely what a good poem means, but of HOW DOES IT MEAN, a process one can come much closer to discussing.

There is a necessary epilogue. Mr. Frost has often discussed this poem on the platform, or more usually in the course of a long evening after a talk. Time and again I have heard him say that he just wrote it off, that it just came to him, and that he set it down as it came.

Once at Bread Loaf, however, I heard him add one very essential piece to the discussion of how it "just came." One night, he said, he had sat down after supper to work at a long piece of blank verse. The piece never worked out, but Mr. Frost found himself so absorbed in it that, when next he looked up, dawn was at his window. He rose, crossed to the window, stood looking out for a few minutes, and *then* it was that "Stopping by Woods" suddenly "just came," so that all he had to do was cross the room and write it down.

Robert Frost is the sort of artist who hides his traces. I know of no Frost work sheets anywhere. If someone has raided his wastebasket in secret, it is possible that such work sheets exist somewhere, but Frost would not willingly allow anything but the finished product to leave him. Almost certainly, therefore, no one will ever know what was in that piece of unsuccessful blank verse he had been working at with such concentration, but I fo one would stake my life that could that work sheet be uncovered, it would be found to contain the germinal stuff of "Stopping by Woods"; that what was a-simmer in him all night without finding its proper form, suddenly, when he let his still-occupied mind look away, came at him from a different direction, offered itself in a different form, and that finding that form exactly right the impulse proceeded to marry itself to the new shape in one of the most miraculous performances of English lyricism.

And that, too — whether or not one can accept so hypothetical a discussion — is part of HOW the poem means. It means that marriage to the perfect form, the poem's shapen declaration of itself, its moment's monument fixed beyond all possibility of change. And thus, finally, in every truly good poem, "How does it mean?" must always be answered "Triumphantly." Whatever the poem "is about," *how* it means is always how Genesis means: the word become a form, and the form become a thing, and — when the becoming is true — the thing become a part of the knowledge and experience of the race forever.

INDEX